STARTING AT THE FINISH LINE

STARTING AT THE FINISH LINE

THE GOSPEL OF GRACE FOR MORMONS

JOHN B. WALLACE

ISBN 13: 978-0-9914622-0-9

Library of Congress Catalog Card Number: 2013912230

CONTENTS

ACKNOWLEDGMENTS

It may sound cliché but I could never have completed this work without the love, support, and invaluable insights of some very special people. To John Morehead and Kim Keller, thank you for encouraging me to tone down the rhetoric a notch or two. I hope it's made for a less contentious book. To my beloved pastor, Brad Young, a heartfelt thanks for your priceless input and for making sure this work passed doctrinal muster. You are truly a man after God's own heart and every bit my spiritual father in this great work. And to Jim Fogg, Justin Arcy, and Brandon Wallace–thanks for not pulling any punches. Many of your suggestions found their way into the narrative.

Finally, a very special thanks to the amazing Carma Naylor. You, more than anyone else, inspired me to write this book. What an honor to count you and Charles as friends.

PREFACE

A couple of years ago, my long-time friend and business partner asked me a provocative question. He said, "John, imagine that you are at the podium of an event being held in a large stadium. This stadium is filled with 75,000 Mormons, every Mormon you've ever known, plus another 65,000 or so. And you've got their undivided attention for twenty minutes. What would you say? What would you do with that opportunity?"

My mind darted in a hundred different directions. Maybe I could share all the different stumbling blocks of Latter-day Saint doctrine I struggled with back when I was a member of the church. Or maybe my time would be best served outlining the various discrepancies in Joseph Smith's accounting of his First Vision or the numerous anachronisms and inconsistencies found in the Book of Mormon. Or how about polygamy, racism, or the Mountain Meadows Massacre? So many things, so little time.

No. If I had just twenty minutes to pour my heart out to these fine people, I would not waste a single minute on any of those issues, not even one syllable. I would focus all of my attention on the finished work of Jesus Christ. I would preach the gospel of grace. I would preach about Christ on the cross, suffering and dying to pay the price for my sin, and about God accepting the substitutionary offering of His Son as payment in full for every sin ever committed and declaring righteous every imperfect sinner that receives Christ and trusts in Him and Him alone for that righteousness—the Divine Exchange. I would share the "good news" of the gospel, the gospel of grace. That's what I would do, and pray that I could do the subject justice in twenty minutes.

I got home that night and roughly sketched out my thoughts on how to explain the good news of the gospel and make it *sound* like good news to devout Latter-day Saints. My thoughts coalesced into an essay that I entitled "The Gospel of Grace (for Mormons)." It was met with high praise and critical acclaim by the two people that read it—my son and a buddy of mine. Eventually, that one question posed by my friend and the notes I jotted down in response to it gave birth to this book.

This was the book I *had* to write. And as the chapters flowed onto these pages, I came to realize that this book has, in fact, been writing itself in my mind for the last eight years. Getting it down on paper seemed only a formality.

Ultimately, I wrote this for my parents. And it is to them that I dedicate every word.

—John B. Wallace
January, 2013

SECTION I
INTRODUCTION

CHAPTER 1

HINDSIGHT IS 20:20

> Train a child up in the way he should go, even when he is old he will not depart from it.
>
> —Proverbs 22:6

Sometime in the fall of 1973, my older sister, who was thirteen at the time, came home from school with cigarettes in her coat pocket. When my mother confronted her with the cigarettes, my sister, in between sobs, cried out, "I just want to be Mormon!"

Three months later, my entire family was baptized into the Church of Jesus Christ of Latter-day Saints (LDS church). But I should probably back up.

My parents were high-school sweethearts in Lawndale, California, inseparable from about the age of twelve. In fact, they were next-door neighbors. Dad literally married the girl next door. My grandparents, therefore, were neighbors and very good friends.

Of my four grandparents, only Ruby, my dad's mom, was much of a churchgoer. In fact, she taught Sunday school in their small Methodist church for many years. Papa (Dad's dad) avoided church at all costs, and my mom's parents were, at best, special occasion churchgoers. However, the religious landscape in our family began to change sometime in 1955. My

Uncle Chuck, Mom's older brother, began hanging out with some of the Mormon kids at his high school and going to Mormon stake dances. He felt comfortable with them and admired what they stood for. Eventually, he investigated the church and, in January of 1956, was baptized. A year later, Grandpa followed suit.

Ironically, it was my grandmother Oleva, my mom's mom, who ended up having the greatest fascination with the Mormon Church. I say it was ironic because she was the one with the greatest impediment to joining the church. She was a chain smoker and had been for decades. She had gained at least the initial rumblings of a testimony of the church and watched her son and husband join, but she simply could not imagine ever giving up her cigarettes.

Then one evening, their local bishop challenged her to pray about the truthfulness of the Book of Mormon, the prophetic calling of Joseph Smith, and the uniqueness of the church as God's "one true church." Then he took it one step further. He challenged her to quit smoking altogether. That night, Grandma got on her knees and took that challenge. When she emerged from her bedroom, she was equipped with two things: a testimony of the church and the will power to stop smoking. She marched into the bathroom, flushed her last pack of cigarettes down the toilet, and never smoked another cigarette in her life! She was baptized shortly thereafter.

For a number of reasons, my parents did not feel inclined to make a serious investigation into the LDS church, despite the conversion of Mom's entire side of the family. They were busy raising three small children. Life was good, for the most part, and they were reasonably content attending their local Methodist church.

After they moved to Long Beach, though, my parents felt the need to find a church closer to home. One of Dad's fire department friends recommended the First Baptist Church of Lakewood, and that's where we attended until 1973—the year that those menacing cigarettes tried to make a comeback in our family.

As it turned out, Janet (my would-be cigarette-smoking sister) loved to sit at the feet of my grandmother while she regaled her with stories of Joseph Smith and the restoration of the church. She literally could not get enough of those stories and, as a little girl, pined for the day when she too could become Mormon. She knew, however, this was not something she could safely share with Mom and Dad. We were Baptists now, and although we were not devout by any stretch (we attended church a couple times a month), my parents saw no compelling reason to change religions—that is, until those cigarettes were discovered in Janet's coat pocket. Structure was what we needed, and structure was what we got.

Thus, after Janet's outburst, and after taking the missionary lessons, we were baptized, all five of us, in February of 1974. I remember clearly the warm waters of the baptismal font and the words that Uncle Chuck spoke over me that day. My life as a Mormon had begun. I was eight years old.

My parents, from the very beginning, were "natural Mormons." I, on the other hand, was a square peg in a round hole; although, to the outside observer (and certainly to every bishop and stake president that ever interviewed me during my youth), I appeared to be the ideal Mormon boy. I was consistent in attending all my Sunday and mid-week meetings, president of every Aaronic Priesthood quorum I was ever in, and arguably the "go-to" kid for the two-minute talk in sacrament meeting. So in truth, my peg *became* square over time.

It all started sometime during my junior year of high school, during a conversation I had with my beloved bishop, who was also my history teacher. I had heard through the grapevine that as Latter-day Saints we believed that God (God the Father, Elohim) was not always God, that he was once a man just like us. Further, I had been told that we mortals, if we were faithful to all the commandments and ordinances of the gospel as taught by the LDS church, could one day become gods ourselves and that we would rule over our own world and populate that world with our own spirit children. I was convinced I must have completely misunderstood this teaching or that it was just another form of Mormon apocrypha, similar to the Adam-God doctrine or reported sightings of the three Nephites. I just needed my trusted bishop and friend to dismiss this for me so I could go on with my day. My other thought was, *If this really were true, why would my parents not have shared this with me? A teaching of this magnitude? Impossible.*

And so one afternoon I approached my bishop in his classroom after school. I knocked on his door, and he invited me in.

"Is it true?" I asked.

"Is what true?"

"Was God really a man like us? Is it possible for men to become gods one day?"

Ordinarily a very free and easy guy, he suddenly appeared uneasy and uncomfortable. A strange, forced smile spread across his face. "You're too young, John, to really be delving into these deeper doctrines," was his reply.

One look from me told him that I was not going to let him off the hook that easily.

My bishop took a deep breath, looked me straight in the eye, and said, "Yes, it's true! This is what Joseph Smith taught shortly before he was martyred, and it is what the church proclaims to this day."

I was stunned. How had I missed this little detail of doctrine? Since my early childhood, I'd always considered God to be an omniscient, powerful, benevolent being who had always been God "from everlasting to everlasting." At no point had I entertained the thought that my God had once been just a regular guy.

More unsettling to me, however, was the idea that there might be some guy named Larry from Des Moines, Iowa, who was next in line to be God on some other planet! With all due respect to my devout Mormon reader, none of this rang true to me.

I remember half walking, half running to the nearest bathroom, where I needed a minute to collect my thoughts. Three distinct thoughts flooded my mind:1) *There is no way this is true.* 2) *Even if it were true, I don't want to be God! I can barely manage my own pitiful, little life.* 3) *How am I going to defend this doctrine for the rest of my life—to anyone who is not LDS?* This was no small matter. This was the most audacious doctrine I had ever heard in my life or ever hoped to hear.

And so, in a matter of five minutes, my reasonably smooth, round peg was whittled into a very distinct and angular square peg. And I knew that there wasn't enough WD-40 in the world to make my square peg fit into the round hole of Mormonism ever again. Looking back, this was the moment in which I went from being a "true believing Mormon" (TBM on blogs these days) to a "cultural Mormon" (CM). From this point forward, it was all a matter of life management. I was going along to get along.

And go along I did. I went on a two-year mission to Buenos Aires, Argentina (District Leader, Zone Leader, over twenty baptisms); graduated Magna Cum Laude from Brigham Young University; was sealed in the Salt Lake temple; became Elders Quorum President in virtually every ward I attended after my mission; etc. I even read the Book of Mormon at least ten times from cover to cover, in three languages; although, I confess that I only understood about 70 percent of what I was reading in Portuguese. In short, I was a home-teaching, tithe-paying, garment-wearing, Word of Wisdom-keeping, temple recommend-holding, "cultural Mormon"—truly the most conflicted of all creatures.

I mention all of this for two reasons. First, for the critic who would dismiss this work as illegitimate because perhaps I never really knew what it meant to be a devout Mormon, I felt the need to establish my legitimacy. My Mormon *bona fides* are (or were) close to impeccable. Some, even within my own family, contend that I have forgotten much about the Mormon faith and no longer have any business writing or lecturing on the subject. If you will forgive my ego for a moment, here's what I say to these, "Anytime, anywhere." I have spent much of the last eight years of my life reading and rereading all things LDS. (The Bible, of course, is something I'm immersed in daily.) As difficult as it has been for me at times, I have reread all three of the LDS standard works, *The Teachings of the Prophet Joseph Smith, Articles of Faith, Jesus the Christ, The Miracle of Forgiveness*, and (for sake of space and time) virtually every other major LDS work published since the days of Nauvoo.

To be fair, I will tell you that I've also read most every scholarly work written by D. Michael Quinn, Fawn Brodie, Todd Compton, Michael Marquardt, Grant Palmer, and many of the other brilliant historians who have devoted their lives to the study of Mormon origins. I owe a tremendous debt of gratitude to these courageous writers who have made an objective, unfiltered search for truth. Needless to say, I do not share in Elder Packer's disdain for historians who "idolize the truth."

Second, and more importantly, I share my personal history simply because I want you to know who I am and who I was. The fact is that I was Mormon for twenty years, and if you add in my formative years at the First Baptist Church, I've been an evangelical Christian for twenty years. I am eminently qualified to write this book, if for no other reason than the concept of salvation as understood by the Latter-day Saints, and salvation as proclaimed in the New Testament—and the migration from the former to the latter—*is* my story! And while I do not want this book to be about me, my story nearly perfectly captures the essence of this migration out of a religion of works and obedience into a relationship (with Christ) of acceptance and freedom.

One final point regarding my qualifications to tackle this subject: I felt no need to co-author this book with any of my devout LDS friends, and I have many. There are some wonderful point-counter point books of this style, and I highly recommend them. (*Bridging the Divide* by Greg Johnson and Robert Millett is my personal favorite.) Most of these books are written by a Mormon and an evangelical Christian. But remember, I have been both. I still speak fluent *Mormonese*, as it were; although, I admit that it no longer feels like my native tongue. Rather, it feels like a foreign language that I learned as a child and now, with a little practice, has come back to me. I can still think and even feel like a Mormon. Also, Mormons are still very much my people—my parents, one of my sisters and her husband, and two of my best friends on the face of this earth(one of which was my missionary companion in Argentina!). This is my inner circle. These are the people I love the most.

People sometimes ask me if I am anti-Mormon. This frustrates me to no end. Anti-Mormon? They must not know me, and they certainly don't know my wonderful parents or my best friends! I love my people. I love Mormons with a love that, unfortunately, they themselves don't always understand.

Even my parents, I fear, see me as being antagonistic toward them and their beliefs. They are exactly *half* right. I am not antagonistic to my parents; I love them. However, I do not believe that Joseph Smith was a prophet of God. I do not believe the Book of Mormon is a legitimate ancient document of historical value. And I do not believe that The Church of Jesus Christ of Latter-day Saints is the "only true church on the face of the earth."

However, despite this disclaimer, let me tell you what this book is not. This book is not a prosecution of Mormonism. This is not my attempt to disprove the Book of Mormon or the prophetic calling of Joseph Smith. We are not going to talk about priesthood authority, temple work, polygamy, or the need for a prophet "to guide us in these latter days." But just as the artist needs a canvas on which to create his painting, I need to brush up against the doctrines of Mormonism as I paint for you the biblical rendition of the gospel of grace.

This book, then, is very simply a defense of that gospel: Christ on the cross, suffering and paying the penalty for our sins, and us, trusting in His sacrifice and His sacrifice *alone* as our salvation—as proclaimed in the New Testament of the Bible.

THIS BOOK, THEN, IS VERY SIMPLY A DEFENSE OF THAT GOSPEL: CHRIST ON THE CROSS, SUFFERING AND PAYING THE PENALTY FOR OUR SINS.

It is axiomatic in football circles that defense wins championships. I agree. If you consider my defense of the cross of Jesus to be an indictment of LDS theology, as I do, then so be it. I believe the supporting evidence is overwhelming.

Ironically (and I say ironically because Mormons nearly always assume the posture of defendant), the gauntlet was thrown down originally by Joseph Smith himself, when he emerged from the Sacred Grove equipped with the notion that essentially all the extant religions were false, corrupt, and unworthy of his association. (For now, we'll ignore the fact that in 1828, Joseph and Emma briefly joined the Methodist church. This was a full eight years after God told him not to.)

Decades later, John Taylor, third president of the church, said this at a General Conference in Salt Lake City (as recorded in Journal of Discourses, Vol. 6, p. 25): "We talk about Christianity, but it is a perfect pack of nonsense … the Devil could not invent a better engine to spread his work than the Christianity of the 19th century." Later he would add, "What does the

Christian world know about God? Nothing ... they know neither God nor the things of God" (Journal of Discourses, Vol. 13, p. 225).

Well now, President Taylor, those are some rather bold and antagonistic claims. Let's try for a moment to remain objective here, for these claims are either true or they are not. Is biblical Christianity—we are saved by grace through faith in Christ—a "pack of nonsense"? Does the Christian indeed know *nothing* about God and His grand work of redemption? For eighteen years, I have stayed out of this fight. I've kept my mouth shut. Now, for whatever reason, God has seen fit to allow me to weigh in. This book is my weigh in.

Before we really dig into the meat of this book, however, I'm going to let you in on a little secret. It might actually save you a lot of time. There is really only one section in this book that matters, and it happens to be the very next section, which I've entitled *A Defense of the Bible.*

Let me explain. The eighth Article of Faith reads, in part, "We believe the Bible to be the word of God, as far as it is translated correctly ..." Therefore, the way I see it, I have one job and one job only: to convince you that the Bible has been, in fact, translated correctly! Let me rephrase that. My job is to invite you, the Latter-day Saint, to research all available evidence (and it is substantial) and come to your *own* conclusion that the Bible has been not only translated correctly but also transmitted down through the centuries with an astonishing degree of accuracy.

Once you are convinced of this, my preference is that you set this comparatively insignificant book down and immerse yourself in the Bible, focusing initially on the New Testament but with an eye also to the prophecies and foreshadowing in the Old Testament. When you do this, you will discover that the Bible is all about the cross of Jesus. It is about God the Son, who took upon himself the form of man and came in to this world to offer Himself as a sacrifice for sin. And it is about helpless, sinful man, who is put in the position of needing to make a choice: do I or do I not trust in this sacrifice in order to be justified and made righteous in the sight of God? The powerful truth of this *divine exchange*, Christ's righteousness gifted to us in exchange for our sinfulness, will explode into your heart and mind by the power of the Holy Spirit, who will indeed "teach you all things" (Jn 14:26). This isn't a burning in the bosom. This is a wildfire that will burn totally out of control within you. I know because I've experienced both the burning and the wild fire.

However, for those of you who may not be convinced of the perfect reliability of the Bible after reading Section II, I ask that you please spend some time with me as I explain to you, in terms I believe you will understand, what the gospel of grace is really all about. Will you open your mind and your heart for a couple of days as you go through these pages? Can you leave your presuppositions behind, just for a little while?

Maybe you're reading this book because you wish to prove me wrong. That's perfectly okay with me. By all means, get out your pen and your highlighter and go to town. I'm tough. I can take it. Frankly, anything that gets the pages of your Bible turning is fine by me.

Realistically, I know who my target audience is, and it probably isn't the true believing Mormon. The totally committed Latter-day Saint would probably only pick up this book in order to throw it in the fireplace as kindling. I get that. I really wrote this book for the Mormon who, in a sense, is going through the motions, who values and enjoys all the wonderful benefits of being a member of the church (and there are many) but who secretly doesn't believe the Joseph Smith narrative in its entirety, if at all. I confess that I wrote the book *I* needed twenty-plus years ago, when I was agonizing over whether to leave the church or not. Well, better late than never.

One final thing before we begin: please know that every word I've written comes from a place of love. I feel the need to say this because I know how I can come across sometimes—combative and borderline cocky (okay, maybe not so borderline). But it's never combativeness for the sake of combat; it's either to make a point or to get your attention. I want to engage you fully in this journey of ideas because it is, I believe, both supremely important and urgent.

My first love is Jesus Christ, and to Him I owe everything. He and He alone has saved me from a life of helplessness and rebellion, as you will soon learn. All praise and glory to my beautiful Savior!

Second, I have a boundless love for my LDS family and friends. I have one desire in all of this: that we all live together in God's glorious kingdom, enjoying forever the riches of eternal life in His presence.

If I have to be knocked around a bit and be the family piñata for a season, I will assume that role gladly. Now, let the fiesta begin!

SECTION II
A DEFENSE OF THE BIBLE

CHAPTER 2

SHE LOVES ME, SHE LOVES ME NOT

> The grass withers, the flower fades, But the word of our God stands forever.
>
> —Isaiah 40:8

The summer before my senior year in high school, I worked in a bee warehouse, owned and operated by the family of my priest quorum adviser. It was a tough gig, extracting honey out of heavy, sticky boxes in a metal warehouse that routinely got up to 120 degrees inside. It was lonely, thankless work. But at least I was making big money: $4.25 an hour! Being the extremely frugal lad that I was, I managed to save right around $1,000 that summer—spending money for my senior year. Not too shabby.

When I got back to school in September, however, I discovered that my good friend Scott had totally outdone me. He had gotten a job at a toilet manufacturing plant in Riverside and managed to save $2,000 (twice my haul). And he did it making toilets! This was totally unacceptable to me.

I did the only thing I could think to do in light of this very disturbing news; I lied. I began telling anyone and everyone that I had earned and saved $2,000. In fact, the lie started when, on the very first day of school, Scott told me about his amazing toilet exploits and how much money he'd saved. In a flash and with very little forethought, I blurted out, "Hey, me too!" And so the lie began. If I had to guess, I probably told that lie fifty times over the next two months, maybe more.

Then, sometime in early November, I went to my local bank in Temecula to withdraw $100 from my savings account. It was the first time I had tapped into my savings that fall; life was extremely busy with early morning seminary, AP classes, and basketball practice every day. Anyway, the teller handed me $100 cash and asked if I'd like a printout of my balance on the account. "Sure, why not?" This is where the life lesson begins.

A quick glance at the statement revealed that I now had approximately $900 in my account. *Hang on just one minute here. Something has gone terribly wrong.* In my mind, I should have had $1,900 in my account after that $100 withdrawal, not $900. There was literally a $1,000 shortfall in my account and I, in no uncertain terms, let my teller know it. She, of course, had only the truth on her side—every deposit in and withdrawal from my account since I opened it a year earlier. We battled verbally for a minute or two, until finally I left in a huff, determined to take the matter up with my parents when I got home. *Surely Dad will sort this out with my inept bank.*

I was fuming as I left the bank, fuming on my walk to the car, and still fuming halfway through my drive home. Then the truth of the matter struck me like a 7-iron. I had lied. I had lied over and over again. I never saved $2,000. It was $1,000. But I had repeated the canard so many times that it had literally become my reality—not actual reality, just my own little, secret reality.

Mormons do this with the Bible. A lie is repeated over and over, namely that the Bible has been altered, contaminated, and not "translated correctly," and it becomes their reality. I am not saying that any given Latter-day Saint *knows* he is lying; rather, I am saying that he is guilty of repeating a lie that, in most cases, was handed down to him. And this isn't exactly a "little white lie." This is a massive distortion of the truth that carries very serious consequences.

It is for this very reason that I am devoting an entire section to a defense of the accuracy and reliability of the Bible. This is necessary for the purposes of this book and important in general. It is necessary because from Chapter 5 on, I will be explaining the gospel of grace as revealed in the Bible. It is important because, to the Christian anyway, *nothing* could be more foundational than establishing the "whole counsel of God" and identifying its source.

Is the Bible the whole counsel of God? Can we place all of our trust in the Bible to lead us to Christ and to teach us exactly how a relationship with Christ saves us eternally in God's kingdom? Yes, we can. In fact, we must.

Let's first explore the untenable and awkward relationship the devout Mormon has with the Bible. Then I will try to help you develop a whole new relationship with that amazing book.

Plain and Precious Truths

Early in 1842, a man by the name of John Wentworth, editor of the *Chicago Democrat*, wrote a letter to Joseph Smith, asking for a basic summary of the founding of the Mormon faith and an overview of the church's beliefs. In response to the latter part of this request, Joseph penned what are now known as the thirteen Articles of Faith, later to be canonized and included in the *Pearl of Great Price*. Perhaps the most controversial of these articles, at least to the devout Bible-believing Christians at that time, was the eighth. It reads, in part, "We believe the Bible to be the word of God *as far as it is translated correctly* ..." (italics mine). And so began the dichotomous, hard-to-reconcile relationship the Latter-day Saints have with the Bible, a relationship that persists to this very day.

Initially, Joseph Smith and the early apostles at least paid lip service to the value of the Bible. In *Teachings of the Prophet Joseph Smith*, we find, "He who reads it oftenest will like it best, and he who is acquainted with it, will know the Hand [of the Lord] wherever he can see it" (p. 56). And a century later, Elder Bruce R. McConkie concedes, "In its present form, the Bible is divided into Old and New Testaments and has a total of 66 books within its covers. These books contain doctrinal, historical, prophetic, and poetic materials of transcendent worth. Members of the Church are commanded to teach the principles of the gospel that are in the Bible" (*Mormon Doctrine*, p. 83).

And finally, in one of the more irreconcilable of all Mormon claims, we read the following in the opening paragraph of the Introduction to the Book of Mormon: "The Book of Mormon is a volume of holy scripture comparable to the Bible. It is a record of God's dealings with the ancient inhabitants of the Americas and contains, *as does the Bible*, the fullness of the everlasting gospel" (italics mine).

So here we read in plain English that according to the publishers of the Book of Mormon, the Bible does, in fact, contain the "fullness of the everlasting gospel." And while you will get no argument from the Christian on this point, you'll see why I say this is an irreconcilable position held by the Latter-day Saints. (So irreconcilable, in fact, that the LDS church has officially removed the phrase "as does the Bible" in the new 2013 edition of the Book of Mormon.) For, alas, just twenty-five pages into the Book of Mormon, we begin to see the full frontal assault on the reliability of the Bible. In 1 Nephi 13:28–29, we read:

> Wherefore, thou seest that after the book hath gone forth through the hands of the great and abominable church, that there are many

> plain and precious things taken away from the book, which is the book of the Lamb of God. And after these plain and precious things were taken away it goeth forth unto all the nations of the Gentiles; and after it goeth forth unto all the nations of the Gentiles, yea, even across the many waters which thou hast seen with the Gentiles which have gone forth out of captivity, thou seest—because of the many plain and precious things which have been taken out of the book, which were plain unto the understanding of the children of men, according to the plainness which is in the Lamb of God—because of these things which are taken away out of the gospel of the Lamb, an exceedingly great many do stumble, yea, insomuch that Satan hath great power over them.

What do we learn from this passage? We learn three things: 1)There is a book that, after it goes through the hands of a great and abominable church, has many plain and precious truths removed from it. 2) This process of deletion/truncation turns what was a clear, easy-to-understand book into something less clear and less plain. 3) These plain and precious truths were apparently of such critical nature, that by their omission, people who read the book began to stumble, lose their way, and ultimately come under the power of Satan. This is no small matter.

The next obvious questions are: Which book are we talking about? What is the identity of this "great and abominable church?" An angel conversing with Nephi answers the first question in 1 Nephi 13:23:

> And he said: Behold it proceedeth out of the mouth of a Jew. And I, Nephi, beheld it; and he said unto me: The book that thou beholdest is a record of the Jews, which contains the covenants of the Lord, which he hath made unto the house of Israel; and it also containeth many of the prophecies of the holy prophets; and it is a record like unto the engravings which are upon the plates of brass, save there are not so many; nevertheless, they contain the covenants of the Lord, which he hath made unto the house of Israel; wherefore, they are of great worth unto the Gentiles.

Clearly the angel is referring here to the Bible, at least to the Old Testament.

As for the identity of this devious church, which, according to verse 26 is "most abominable above all other churches," the LDS church definitively identified it as the Roman Catholic Church—that is until 1966, when Elder McConkie was asked to remove this designation from his encyclopedic work, *Mormon Doctrine*. Today you would be hard pressed to find a General Authority willing to make such a positive identification.

In any event, 1 Nephi 13 provides the Latter-day Saints with scriptural support for their claim that the Bible was contaminated, edited, and perverted to such an extent that it actually became and *still is* an instrument used by Satan to lead people astray. (They also say this because it was never fully rectified [by Joseph Smith].)That is quite an assertion. So, have the LDS prophets and apostles softened their stance on the Bible since the publication of the Book of Mormon in 1830? You tell me.

Joseph Smith wrote, "I believe the Bible as it read when it came from the hand of the original writers. Ignorant translators, careless transcribers, or designing and corrupt priests have committed many errors" (*TPJS*, p. 327). This seems to cover the gamut pretty well—translators, who didn't really know what they were doing; transcribers, who knew what they were doing but were just being sloppy; and finally, corrupt priests (workers of Satan), who knew very well what they were doing in removing the "plain and precious truths" that would presumably lead one to Christ!

Surely *some* of the good stuff was left in the Bible, right? After all, it is canonized scripture, one of the four standard works of the LDS church.

Orson Pratt, an early apostle of the church and close confidant of Joseph Smith, didn't think so. Pratt once declared, "Who in his right mind could, for one moment, suppose the Bible in its present form to be a perfect guide. Who knows that even one verse of the Bible has escaped pollution" (*Journal of Discourses*, v. 18, p. 172).

Most Mormons are aware that many of the early leaders of the church, Orson Pratt included, were often given to hyperbole. For example, Joseph Smith, in his headier days in Nauvoo, once boasted that he had done something that even Jesus couldn't do: hold a church together. When I was a member of the church, these statements always made me cringe. This last quote by Orson Pratt sort of falls into the same category for many. But certainly the church has softened its stance on the contamination of the Bible since the 1830s, right? Again, you tell me.

In his book *Millenial Messiah*, published in 1982, Elder McConkie drove the proverbial nail in the Bible's coffin with one concise statement. Really it is just a paraphrasing of 1 Nephi 13:29: "Satan guided his servants in taking many plain and precious things from the Bible, so that men would stumble and lose their souls" (p. 161).

So, if we are to understand Elder McConkie correctly, Satan himself has wrested control of the Bible and made it an instrument to serve *his* purpose, which is to cause people to lose their souls. No wonder the introduction to the Book of Mormon includes this quote from Joseph Smith: "I told the brethren that the Book of Mormon was the most correct of any book on earth, and the keystone of our religion, and a man would get nearer to God by abiding by its precepts, than by any other book."

It is certainly easy to see why the Bible could never be the keystone of the Mormon religion, not with all the "deletions" and "corruptions" it has endured. In the final analysis, Latter-day Saints believe the Bible to be unreliable, incomplete, insufficient, corrupted, and ultimately inferior (to the Book of Mormon). Gee, with friends like the Bible, who needs enemies?

And yet, the last time I checked, The Holy Bible (King James Version), is still canonized LDS scripture, still one of the four standard works! Can someone please help me understand this? Am I missing something? Is the Bible the Word of God or an instrument of Satan? Or is it both, as the Latter-day Saints seem to be implying? And if both, how might I ferret out the good stuff and dance around the mine fields of false, Satan-tampered stuff? And how can the LDS church, or any church for that matter, teach from a book that they believe was altered by the devil in order to lead them astray?

IS THE BIBLE THE WORD OF GOD OR AN INSTRUMENT OF SATAN?

The Builder and the Blueprints

Imagine, if you will, a general contractor who specializes in building high-rise commercial buildings. This well-respected man wins a contract to build a skyscraper in New York City. He receives the blueprints, assembles his team of subcontractors, and begins construction. The site is leveled, the foundation poured, and within a couple months, you can begin to appreciate the enormity of this structure. It has large, steel girders; millions of pounds of concrete; endless miles of wires and piping. Then one day, as the general contractor is overseeing the placement of some large, steel beams, which are being cantilevered out to provide terraces at different levels, and they are about to rivet everything in place, the head structural engineer arrives at the site.

"Hold on there!" he barks. "What are you doing?"

"Placing beams for the terraces," responds the contractor.

"And how long are those beams?" the engineer asks.

"Thirty feet, exactly according to specs," the contractor confidently replies.

The engineer shakes his head in disbelief. "Absolutely not! Got to be thirty-five. Thirty-five and no shorter," he insists.

The contractor pulls out the master blueprints and jabs his index finger three times for effect right where it says the beams are to be thirty feet long.

"Well," the engineer replies, "you can't believe everything you read in the blueprints. Obviously someone messed with the plans, because I'm telling you they're thirty-five. And I should know. I helped design this building!"

Well, on one hand, the contractor is relieved that the engineer was there to correct this mistake. The last thing he wants to do is build a structure where fifty people plummet to their death off a terrace that has inadequate support! On the other hand, he's left wondering what other critical errors might be lurking in the blueprints.

Sure enough, a few weeks later, the lead engineer points out that the concrete floors have to be 24" thick, not the 18" specified in the plans! Later, it's something else.

My question is: at what point in our story does the general contractor call "time out" and demand some blueprints that he can trust? The most likely scenario, of course, is that he would have pulled the plug on this project after discovering the *first* significant error in the plans, if for no other reason than his own liability. Right?

My advice to the Mormon church, not that anyone has asked me for it, would be this: make up your mind about the reliability of the Bible. Either embrace it as the infallible, inspired Word of God (as the rest of the Christian world has) or just chuck it once and for all. Your prophet already declared that the Bible is *not* the keystone of your religion. He's given you ample cover to just focus your teachings on the Book of Mormon. After all, when you have the "most correct of any book on earth" in your canon, why even trifle with anything of lesser value? It makes no sense. It would be like owning a Ferrari and yet driving around in your old clunker.

My LDS reader knows as well as I do, however, that the Mormon Church is not going to discard the Bible any time soon. Rather, the Latter-day Saints appear content to cherry pick the Bible. For example, when the devout Mormon encounters verses like Ephesians 2:8–9, which says that we are saved by grace, through faith, and that this salvation is not *at all* by works (so that no man can boast), he simply labels this passage as one that was not "translated correctly." On the other hand, when he reads Matthew 5:48, where Jesus invites his followers to "be ye therefore perfect even as my Father in heaven is perfect," his heart soars. Apparently *that's* one of the good ones that escaped translational error. See how this works? I did it all the time when I was a missionary in Argentina. Heads I win; tails you lose.

Now, that's about as prosecutorial as I get. I promised you a *defense* of the Bible, and a defense you shall receive, because here's the good news for my LDS friends: the Bible is the infallible, inspired Word of God! Jesus proclaimed, "Heaven and earth will pass away, but my word will not pass away" (Mt 24:25).

I am trying to imagine Jesus not making good on this promise. I am trying to imagine a world in which God cannot protect His own holy writ from the mischievous hands of our common enemy. Personally, I don't need scholars or clergymen to help me trust in the reliability of the Bible. I have experienced (and continue to experience daily) the rich spiritual feast that is available to me through the Bible. The Bible is the banquet table; eternal life, through Christ, is the spread.

THE BIBLE IS THE BANQUET TABLE; ETERNAL LIFE, THROUGH CHRIST, IS THE SPREAD.

And so, let's revisit the eighth Article of Faith: "We believe the Bible to be the word of God as far as it is translated correctly ..." By Joseph Smith's own assessment, if we could somehow demonstrate that the Bible has, in fact, been translated correctly and transmitted accurately down through the centuries, then we could all come to an agreement that it is the Word of God. And if it is the Word of God, then we can confidently stand upon its teachings, promises, and prophesies. Agreed?

I am supremely confident that the serious seeker of truth will come to this very conclusion once confronted with the facts. There is overwhelming evidence—paleographic, archaeological, inscriptional evidence—as well as fulfilled prophecies that serve to authenticate the Bible beyond any reasonable doubt. Interestingly, even secular, atheistic historians do not necessarily doubt the accuracy of the biblical text! They discount the Bible based on their materialistic/naturalistic world view; that is to say, there is no God, and therefore, there can be no miracles. So, anytime they read of a sea being parted or water being turned to wine, they see this as an indication that the biblical narrative is pure fantasy.

In these next two chapters, we will begin to look at the evidence that supports the reliability of our modern Bible. We will start with the New Testament and then look at the Old Testament. I want to save the best for last.

CHAPTER 3

THE NEW TESTAMENT

> This is the disciple who is testifying to these things and wrote these things, and we know his testimony is true.
>
> —John 21:24

Paleographers, experts in the study of ancient writings and inscriptions, use five universal criteria when assessing the authenticity of an ancient manuscript. In his landmark text *An Introduction to Research in English Literary History*, Dr. Chauncey Sanders lists these as:

1. Documentary style
2. Reliable transmission
3. Early composition
4. External corroboration
5. Character of witnesses

For example, let's say we were interested in verifying the authenticity of the Declaration of Independence and other related documents of the American Revolution. We would start by assessing the style in which the Declaration was written, starting with the opening: "When in the course of human events …" Are we to understand these as actual human events, or was it written in the style of fiction? Is this reality or allegory? Clearly, these were thirteen American colonies declaring real grievances against what they perceived as an oppressive (and very real) governing power, Great Britain.

Then, we check to see if the document has been transmitted to us in a reliable fashion. In this case, we have the original Declaration of Independence, and it is on display in Independence Hall in Philadelphia. It doesn't get any more reliable than that.

Next we ask: Is there much of a chronological gap between the events in question and the original manuscript? And, for that matter, is there a significant chronological gap between the writing of the original manuscript and the oldest available copies? Again, in this case, there is no gap whatsoever. The Declaration was signed on July 4, 1776, at the zenith of colonial frustration with British rule. And because we have the original document, with the actual ink right off the quill of John Hancock, et al, we can stand firm on our knowledge of early composition.

How about external, corroborating evidence of the American Revolution? Obviously, we have a wealth of historical evidence attesting to the reality of this event. There really is an Old North Church in Boston, from which Paul Revere took off on his famous midnight ride. There really is a Fort Ticonderoga at the south end of Lake Champlain in upstate New York. You can visit the fort seven days a week, and for $17.50, you can learn all about how Ethan Allen and his Green Mountain Boys captured it from the Brits in May, 1775.

But to the hard-core skeptic of the American Revolution (as if one actually existed), I would recommend a visit to Independence Hall itself. You can stand right where the founding fathers of this nation signed the document in question. You can see the Liberty Bell right up close, crack and all. Ultimately, you can see for yourself the original Declaration of Independence on display. It's guarded under impenetrable plexiglass but is awe-inspiring nonetheless.

Finally, are the signers of the Declaration reliable sources of historical information? Are they reliable witnesses to the events of the Revolution? Did they have intimate knowledge of the people, places, and things in and around colonial America at that specific moment in time? Did John Hancock, Thomas Jefferson, John Adams, Benjamin Franklin, or James Madison say or do anything during the remainder of their lives to cast doubt upon the historicity of the American Revolution? Of course not. In fact, their lives reflected a perpetuation of the very principles for which they revolted in the first place.

Now, let's apply these same criteria to evaluating the authenticity and accuracy of the New Testament. Actually, let's save some time by ignoring the first and fifth criteria—documentary style and character of witness—and focus our attention on the other three. We can do this, I think, because both Mormons and evangelical Christians agree that the Bible is a legitimate, historical document of God's dealings with the ancient Hebrews and of the life, death, and resurrection of Jesus Christ (and the church era that ensued). Furthermore, I'm fairly certain none of us doubt the character or integrity of Moses, Isaiah, Daniel, Luke, or Paul. So, let's focus our attention on reliable transmission, early composition, and external corroboration.

Before we proceed, though, I need to ask my LDS reader one question. Did you arrive at the conclusions that the Bible is unreliable as a historical text because it has translational errors and that plain and precious truths have been removed from it after looking at the text itself and all the corroborating evidence? Or have you come to the biblical text with a presupposition? Have you held to the belief that the Bible is inaccurate because you've been told that, or have you looked at all the evidence and weighed it out yourself? In these next two chapters, I am asking you to do the latter.

Reliable Transmission

You've probably heard it said that the Bible is the number-one best-seller of all time. There is really no close second. As it turns out, the works of the New Testament were the most frequently copied and widely circulated books of antiquity. Currently, we have 5,686 known Greek manuscripts of the New Testament. We also have over 10,000 Latin Vulgate manuscripts and over 9,000 other early versions in various languages. In total, we have close to 25,000 manuscripts of the New Testament!

To give you some idea about how impressive this number is, Homer's *Iliad* has the second-most number of manuscripts, with only 643 manuscripts still in existence today. And what about the works of Tacitus, considered to be the greatest of all Roman historians? Twenty copies have survived to this day. How about Caesar's *Gallic Wars*? There are ten copies. And yet no one questions the reliability of these ancient works; they are taught in every university in the world without the slightest reservation.

Internationally acclaimed scholar and attorney John Warwick Montgomery summarizes it this way: "To be skeptical of the resultant text of the New Testament books is to allow all of the classical antiquity to slip into obscurity, for no documents of the ancient period are as well attested bibliographically as the New Testament" (Montgomery, *History and Christianity*, 29).

Why is this important? The simplest answer is that 25,000 manuscripts can't be wrong. With such a wealth of documentary resources, scholars from all over the world (many of whom are not Christian) have had the luxury of comparing, analyzing, and dissecting these New Testament manuscripts for hundreds of years. One after the other, the finest scholars in the world have come forward with their summations.

25,000 MANUSCRIPTS CAN'T BE WRONG.

W.F. Albright, considered the dean of biblical archaeology, writes, "No other work from the Graeco-Roman antiquity is so well attested by manuscript tradition as the New Testament. There are many more early manuscripts of the New Testament than there are of any classical author, and the oldest extensive remains of it date only about two centuries after their original composition" (Albright, *The Archaeology of Palestine*, 238).

W. Edward Glenny, professor of New Testament studies at Northwestern College, reports, "God has given us 5,656 manuscripts containing all or parts of the Greek NT. It is the most remarkably preserved book in the ancient world. Not only do we have a great number of manuscripts but they are very close in time to the originals they represent" (Glenny, *PS*, 84).

And F.F. Bruce, the world's foremost Bible scholar, adds this, "There is no body of ancient literature in the world which enjoys such a wealth of good textual attestation as the New Testament" (Bruce, *The Books and the Parchments*, 178).

"THERE IS NO BODY OF ANCIENT LITERATURE IN THE WORLD WHICH ENJOYS SUCH A WEALTH OF GOOD TEXTUAL ATTESTATION AS THE NEW TESTAMENT."

I would like to encourage my LDS readers to do their own research with regards to these manuscripts. Take an hour or two and Google *Codex Vaticanus*, *Codex Sinaiticus*, *Chester Beatty Papyri*, and the *John Ryland's MS*. You will come away with a whole new confidence in and appreciation for the reliability of the New Testament.

Early Composition

Speaking of the *John Ryland's MS*, let's talk about the importance of early composition. By early composition, I mean the space of time between the writing of a historical document and the occurrence of the actual events in question.

If I were to ask you where you were on the morning of September 11, 2001, when you first heard that a commercial airliner had slammed into one of the World Trade Center towers, could you tell me? Could you tell me how you heard the news and how you felt at that moment? Of course you could. But that was twelve years ago. Wouldn't it be reasonable to assert that maybe your memory is a bit clouded about that morning? No, because that was no ordinary morning. For most Americans, it ranks right up there with the Japanese attack on Pearl Harbor on December 7, 1941. These events produce indelible memories.

It has been well established that the Synoptic Gospels, the Gospel of John, Acts (of the apostles), the Pauline letters, and other New Testament books were written between A.D. 50 and A.D. 70. One of the primary reasons these writings are placed prior to A.D. 70 is that there is no mention anywhere in the New Testament of the destruction of Jerusalem by the Romans in that year. This, of course, was a devastating event for all those living in Judea at that time—a total "game-changer." Had any of the New Testament books been written after A.D. 70, they most certainly would have mentioned this event.

And so here's my point: if we accept that the death and resurrection of Jesus occurred in A.D. 32 (or 33), then the accounts of His life and the letters that expound upon His teachings were all written approximately seventeen to thirty-five years after these events! Too far removed, you say? I'm not so sure.

I had a patient last week who told me that if his sweetheart were still alive today, they would be celebrating their seventy-fifth wedding anniversary (he's ninety-three). Since I'm always interested in old folks' stories of their youth, I asked him how the two of them met. His eyes lit up, and he proceeded to share with me, in exquisite detail, their amazing love-at-first-sight story. He even remembered the color of the dress she was wearing that day! It was over seventy-five years ago, and yet, to him, it was like yesterday.

I do not mean any disrespect towards my good friend here, but I think the dramatic events surrounding the death and resurrection of Jesus would be even more memorable, don't you?

Let's return to *John Ryland's Manuscript*. Experts now consider this to be the oldest extant copy of any portion of the New Testament (in this case, the Gospel of John), placing it somewhere between A.D. 90 and A.D. 120. That's pretty early, folks. It is certainly far earlier than the formation of the "great and abominable church," which didn't come along until the mid-fourth century A.D.

Before we leave this segment, though, let me add one more piece to this important puzzle. Did you know that even if we did not have *any* surviving manuscripts of the New Testament (and again, there are nearly 25,000), we could still assemble an accurate text based on the extensive writings of the early church fathers (Justin Martyr, Irenaeus, Clement, Tertullian, etc.)? From their writings, we have over 36,000 well-preserved quotations directly from the New Testament. As J. Harold Greenlee points out, "These quotations are so extensive that the New Testament could virtually be reconstructed from them without the use of New Testament Manuscripts" (Greenlee, *Introduction to New Testament Textual Criticism*, 54).

External Corroboration

And now for the *really* exciting stuff. Whenever we are looking to verify the historical accuracy of an ancient document, external corroborating evidence is weighed very heavily. The New Testament, once again, enjoys an embarrassment of riches when it comes to this kind of corroboration. In this section, we will limit our discussion to just two of the many extra-biblical historians (men with no motive whatsoever to authenticate the events of Jesus' life) and a couple key archaeological discoveries. Please know that we are merely scratching the surface here.

Of the extra-biblical writers, none is more universally respected than Tacitus, a first-century Roman historian said to be *the* most accurate historian of the ancient world. Here he gives an account of the great fire of Rome, for which many held Nero responsible:

> Consequently, to get rid of the report, Nero fastened the guilt and inflicted the most exquisite tortures on a class hated for their abominations, called Christians by the populace. Christus, from whom the name had its origin, suffered the extreme penalty during their reign of Tiberius at the hands of one of our procurators, Pontius Pilate, and a most mischievous superstition, thus checked for the moment, again broke out not only in Judea, the first source of the evil, but even in Rome, where all things hideous and shameful from every part of the world find their center and become popular.
>
> —Tacitus, *Annals*, 15:44

What can we cultivate from this passage? First, Tacitus situates several key people and events in a very specific place and time. During the reign of Tiberius (14 A.D. to 37 A.D.), a man named Christus (Christ) suffered the "extreme penalty" at the hands of a procurator, Pontius Pilate. We also learn that a "mischievous superstition" arose from Judea, clearly in relation to this Christus, and then spread to Rome. Tacitus doesn't specify what this superstition is, but most Bible scholars agree that it is most likely referring to the miraculous resurrection of Jesus Christ and the fact that He appeared to many in Jerusalem after His certain death.

What possible motive would Tacitus have for documenting this phenomenon, especially in light of his personal distaste for this "superstition" as being "hideous and shameful"? The answer is: none whatsoever. This is powerful evidence of the central event in the New Testament narrative.

And now we turn our attention to the prodigious Roman historian Flavius Josephus (A.D. 37 to A.D. 100). Josephus was actually a Jewish Pharisee, who, after surrendering to a Roman regiment that killed off his comrades, came under the employ of the Roman Empire. He wrote two major works of history, *Antiquities of the Jews* and *Jewish Wars*. He also wrote a minor work entitled *Against Apion*.

The writings of Josephus provide us with a treasure trove of corroborating evidence for both the biblical narrative and the constitution of the Bible. To this last point, Josephus clearly identifies the thirty-nine books of the Old Testament and even names them. These thirty-nine books correlate exactly with the Protestant view of the canon of the Old Testament—as opposed to the Roman Catholic view, which respects and includes certain Old Testament Apocrypha.

Additionally, Josephus makes reference to the prophet Daniel and marvels at the accuracy of Daniel's predictions regarding the rise and fall of the Babylonian, Medo-Persian, and Greek empires. Little did he know that his very own Roman empire would be, according to Daniel, the next great world power to fall. In any event, what's important is that Josephus confirms the sixth-century B.C. writing of the book of Daniel. Tuck this little gem away for now, because it will become even more significant to you when we look at the reliability of the Old Testament.

Finally, Josephus wrote one of the most astounding extra-biblical attestations of the life, death, and legacy of Jesus Christ ever recorded. This passage is simply breathtaking in its implications.:

> At this time there was a wise man who was called Jesus. And his conduct was good and [He] was known to be virtuous. Many people from among the Jews and other nations became his disciples. Pilate condemned him to be crucified and to die. And those who have become his disciples do not abandon his discipleship.

> They reported that he had appeared to them three days after his crucifixion and that he was alive; accordingly, he was perhaps the messiah concerning whom the prophets have recounted wonders. (Arabic MS *Kitab Al-Unwan*)

I am hoping that even this small sampling of extra-biblical writings is helping you appreciate the bigger picture and see that the New Testament is an accurate, reliable, historical record of real people and real events.

For a more thorough investigation of these claims, I recommend two excellent sources; although, there are many to choose from. For a concise, well-referenced book on the reliability of the Bible, read Josh McDowell's *The New Evidence That Demands a Verdict*. Part one of his book, "The Case for the Bible," is especially helpful and relevant to our discussion. And for a real-time look at all the archaeological discoveries being made that, time after time, verify the reliability of the Bible, subscribe to *Biblical Archaeological Review*. I've been getting *BAR* for ten years now, and it never fails to amaze me.

Archaeological Evidence

A prodigious amount of archaeological evidence has been pouring in over the past 200 years or so that further confirms many of the people, places, and events in the New Testament narrative. Again, we only have time for a few brief examples.

In November, 1990, researchers uncovered a phenomenally preserved relic now known as the Caiaphas ossuary. An ossuary was an ornate stone box used to hold and preserve the bones of dignitaries in and around Jerusalem between B.C. 20 and A.D. 70, when this practice was discontinued. Caiaphas, of course, was a principle adversary of Jesus and the High Priest in Judea at the time of Jesus' trial and crucifixion. For years, skeptics of the Bible doubted even the existence of the key figures surrounding the life and death of Jesus (including Jesus Himself). But finds like these have served to silence those critics.

About ten years ago, an even more significant ossuary was discovered called the James ossuary. The inscription on the side of this box reads: "James, son of Joseph, brother of Jesus." Skeptics have called the James ossuary a hoax, insisting that the inscription is a forgery. The one thing they haven't quite been able to explain away, however, is the patina (soil residue) found within the letters of the inscription. This patina has been thoroughly analyzed by several independent research teams and found to be 2,000 years old. Well, if the residue in the letters is 2,000 years old, the letters themselves have to be older still. There is no other explanation. So here we have a powerful attestation to not only the half-brother of Jesus but also to Jesus Himself! (The statistical odds that there would have been another James in or around Jerusalem with a father named Joseph and a brother named Jesus—famous enough to have been included in the inscription—are exceedingly small.)

Archaeologists have also uncovered evidence of such people and places as King Herod, Pontius Pilate, Peter (the disciple of Jesus), the Pool of Siloam, the Pool of Bethesda (with all five porticoes described in John 5), the synagogue at Capernaum, and much, much more.

But I want to leave you with this one last example of corroborating archaeological evidence for the New Testament. At first blush, it seems rather insignificant, but I believe the implications are far-reaching.

Those familiar with the book of Acts will recall that during Paul's voyage to Italy (to stand trial in Rome), he and Luke, along with other prisoners, the captain, and the crew, endured a tremendous storm that nearly cost them all their lives. Ultimately, they were shipwrecked on the island of Malta, in the Mediterranean Sea. We pick up the narrative now in Acts 28:1–2 and 7–10 (italics are mine):

> When they had been brought safely through, then we found out that the island was called Malta. The natives showed us extraordinary kindness; for because of the rain that had set in and because of the cold, they kindled a fire and received us all. Now in the neighborhood of that place were lands belonging to the *leading man of the island, named Publius*, who welcomed us and entertained us courteously three days. And it happened that the father of Publius was lying in bed afflicted with recurrent fever and dysentery; and Paul went in to see him and after he had prayed, he laid his hands on him and healed him. After this had happened, the rest of the people on the island who had diseases were coming to him and getting cured. They also honored us with many marks of respect; and when we were setting sail, they supplied us with all we needed.

So, a gracious and generous man on the island of Malta, by the name of Publius, is identified by Luke. Luke tells us that Publius holds the title of "leading man of the island," a sort of strange and simplistic title, to be sure. Bible critics for years dismissed this particular story in Acts because of this seemingly non-historic title given to this so-called Publius. He's not Governor or Legate or Proconsul. He's "leading man of the island."

In the story, it turns out that the father of Publius is deathly ill. Paul lays hands on him and miraculously heals him, as well as many other sick people on the island. If Paul hadn't ingratiated himself to the people of Malta before, he sure had now.

So why is this story so compelling? Because recently, archaeologists have unearthed an authentic first-century inscription in Malta that reads: "Publius, leading man of the island." No one questions the existence of Publius anymore.

But I see a much bigger story here. If Luke was accurate in his description of the shipwreck on Malta and accurate in his identification of Publius as the head honcho of that island, wouldn't it be reasonable to believe Luke's description of Paul's miraculous healing of Publius's father too? And if Paul truly healed all those people by the power of God, could we not also conclude that Paul was a true apostle sent by God? And if a true apostle, can we then trust in his inspired writings—his letters to the Romans, Ephesians, Galatians, etc.? I believe we can. And I hope that you, my LDS reader, agree with me on this, because much of our discussion of the gospel of grace comes from the Pauline letters.

Do all of these manuscripts and archaeological evidences excite you and stir within you a renewed passion for and confidence in the Bible? They should.

Let me ask you another question. What would your reaction be if a similar archaeological find were discovered in, say, Guatemala, a stone inscription that reads, "I, King Limhi, leader of the city of Nephi, bestow great honor upon my chief captain, Gideon, for his valiant defense against the warring Lamanites"? In short order, the entire Mormon world would be abuzz with this astounding archaeological proof of the narrative found in Mosiah 20. Who would you call first? How electrifying would this be for you? I already know the answer. Remember, I was Mormon for twenty years. I just wanted you to imagine this scenario.

My question is: do you feel this same excitement (the excitement you *would* feel in the above scenario) when you read about discoveries authenticating the Bible? If not, why not? Could it be because these discoveries validate general Christian claims and not esoteric LDS claims? Latter-day Saints now want to be included as another Christian iteration—in stark contrast to the isolationism of the early church. Mormon leaders are much more inclined now to say, "We're Christian but different." But if this were the case, it seems to me that Latter-day Saints would be equally excited about these amazing corroborative evidences of the Bible. But the fact is, they're not.

Meanwhile, back at Brigham Young University, there is an entire department devoted to "Book of Mormon archaeology." Could there be a tougher assignment in all of academia? I doubt it, because as of this writing (and a good, solid 183 years since the publication of the Book of Mormon), we have not one artifact, not one inscription, not one single piece of specific archaeological evidence to support the historicity of the Book of Mormon. Nothing. Even so, most Latter-day Saints are inclined to place their full trust in the historical reliability of the Book of Mormon, despite its utter lack of corroborating evidence, and cast doubt upon the reliability of the Bible, with its veritable mountain of evidence.

For example, Joseph Smith claims to have uncovered, at the direction of the angel Moroni, the golden plates on which the Book of Mormon was inscribed, in a stone box at the Hill Cumorah (so named by the Nephites), located between Manchester and Palmyra, New York. Smith also made it clear that Cumorah was the very place where the last great battle between the Nephites and the Lamanites occurred, leading to the extermination of the Nephite tribe. Presumably, hundreds of thousands of men perished in this place. Yet not one single implement of war has ever been discovered there—no spears, no breastplates, nothing at all. No bones have been found either. And we're not exactly talking B.C. 2,500. The Book of Mormon pegs this last great battle at A.D. 421. We know the time and the place, and yet there is no corroborating evidence whatsoever. Does this bother you? If not, why not?

As a continued defense for the Bible, let's now turn our attention to the spectacular evidence that authenticates the Old Testament.

CHAPTER 4

THE OLD TESTAMENT

> Every word of God is tested; He is a shield to those who take refuge in Him.
>
> —Proverbs 30:5

Let's look at the historical reliability of the Old Testament in a fashion similar to how we looked at the New Testament—but with a little twist. Again, because I think we all agree that the Old Testament was written in documentary style (literally a history of the ancient Hebrews) and because none of us doubt the integrity of Moses, Isaiah, Daniel or the rest, we can forgo a discussion of the character of these witnesses. But because of the uniqueness of the Old Testament, I would like to replace these two criteria with two new ones: prophecy and the attestations of Jesus in the New Testament. In fact, let's start with these two.

Prophecy

It is clearly not within the scope of this book to make a thorough examination of the staggering number of already-fulfilled ancient prophecies found in the Old Testament; although, that is a very worthwhile endeavor. I highly recommend John Walvoord's *Major Bible Prophecies* for anyone who has an interest researching this. You will walk away from Dr. Walvoord's book with a deeper trust in God's sovereignty and a profound awe for the role prophecy plays in the self-authentication of the Bible. But since we're here, let's just look at two examples of how the Old Testament proves its own divine origin through its audacious (and accurate) predictions.

THE OLD TESTAMENT PROVES ITS OWN DIVINE ORIGIN THROUGH ITS AUDACIOUS (AND ACCURATE) PREDICTIONS.

In the previous chapter, I made brief mention of Daniel's impressive prophecies regarding the rise and fall of four consecutive world empires: the Babylonian, Medo-Persian, Greek, and Roman empires. He predicted the Medo-Persian conquest of the Babylonian empire hours before it happened, and then, with equal adroitness, he prophesied the fall of the Medo-Persians to the Greeks, which would not take place for another 200 years. He described Alexander the Great to a tee and even described how, upon Alexander's death, the Greek empire would be divided up into four subkingdoms from the north, south, east, and west. This, of course, is precisely what happened.

King Nebuchadnezzar (of Babylon), having heard of Daniel's prodigious abilities to unravel mysteries, asked Daniel if he could make known his disturbing dream and give him a reliable interpretation. Daniel's response revealed not only his remarkable humility but also his utter dependence on God as the source of his wisdom and prophetic powers. We read in Daniel 2:27–30 the following:

> Daniel answered before the king and said, "As for the mystery about which the king has inquired, neither wise men, conjurers, magicians nor diviners are able to declare it to the king. However, there is a God in heaven who reveals mysteries, and He has made known to King Nebuchadnezzar what will take place in the latter days ... But as for me, this mystery has not been revealed to me for any wisdom residing in me more than in any other living man, but for the purpose of making the interpretation known to the king, and that you may understand the thoughts of your mind."

Indeed, God was busy revealing mysteries through His prophet Daniel. In what might be the most astonishing, detailed, and accurate prophecy of the entire Old Testament, Daniel reveals a sweeping view of the future of the House of Israel, in what has come to be known as the "seventy weeks" prophecy found in Daniel 9:24–27. In this prophecy (written sometime around B.C. 535), we learn of the decree to rebuild Jerusalem (B.C. 445), the arrival of Messiah in Jerusalem (A.D. 30), the death of that Messiah, the destruction of Jerusalem (A.D. 70), and finally, the arrival at a later time of an evil ruler who will make a seven-year peace treaty with Israel, only to break the treaty and desecrate a future temple.

As if this weren't impressive enough, did you know that in this prophecy, Daniel predicts Christ's triumphal entry into Jerusalem *to the very day*—not just the month or the year, the very day. He predicted it 567 years in advance! Now, to the secular (non-believing) scholar, there can be only one explanation for this: someone tampered with the text *ex-post facto*. However, for those of us who believe that God, who, outside of space and time, sees past, present, and future as one continuous realm, revealed His mysteries to ancient prophets, it's easy to see the supernatural on display here. For our purposes, it is powerful, undeniable evidence of the reliability of the Old Testament.

And then there's Isaiah. I wish we had time to go through the whole book of Isaiah, but sadly, we cannot. We'll have to limit ourselves to two premium examples of God revealing the reality of Christ through Isaiah—over 700 years in advance.

Isaiah 7:14 reads, "Therefore the Lord Himself will give you a sign: Behold, a virgin will be with child and bear a son, and she will call His name Immanuel." *Immanuel* in Hebrew means "God with us" and clearly refers to the miraculous birth of Christ. If you grew up believing in the prophecies of the Bible, it's easy to take these amazing passages for granted. But when you really stop and consider the implications of verses like this, it should have the effect of solidifying your trust in the text itself.

And then, of course, we have the most extensive (and heart-wrenching) messianic prophecy of the Old Testament in Isaiah 53. In verses 4 and 5 we read, "Surely our griefs He Himself bore, and our sorrows He carried; yet we ourselves esteemed Him stricken, smitten of God, and afflicted. But He was pierced through for our transgressions, He was crushed for our iniquities; the chastening for our well-being fell upon Him, and by His scourging we are healed."

The already-fulfilled prophecies of the Old Testament testify to its reliability. There may not be any more powerful evidence than that.

Attestations of Jesus

The New Testament is full of references to Old Testament events, teachings, and prophecies. One such reference is based on a passage found in Numbers 21:5–9. Here we read a rather bizarre story of how Moses was commanded to lift up a bronze snake on a pole so that all those who had been bitten by poisonous snakes could, by simply looking upon it, be healed of the deadly effects of the venom. One might be tempted to chalk this story up to Old Testament folklore, a strange, forgettable event that may or may not have even happened as described. However, in Jesus' now famous middle-of-the-night dialogue with Nicodemus, we find Him definitively affirming both the historicity of this episode and its meaning. In John 3:14–15, we read, "As Moses lifted up the serpent in the wilderness, even so must the Son of Man be lifted up; so that whoever believes will in Him have eternal life."

Jesus also makes special mention of Daniel, Isaiah, and several other Old Testament prophets, affirming both the authority and fulfillment of their prophecies.

For those interested in learning more about New Testament attestations of Old Testament events, I highly recommend Geisler and Nix's *From God to Us: How We Got Our Bible.* They list over three dozen specific examples, ranging from the translation of Enoch (Heb 11:5) to Jonah in the belly of the fish (Matt. 12:40) to Daniel in the lion's den (Heb 11:33).

External Corroboration

A wealth of archaeological evidence serves to verify the reliability of the Old Testament narrative. There are literally thousands of artifacts and inscriptions to choose from. Let's just look at one prime example.

Perhaps the most astounding archaeological discovery in the twentieth century, in terms of confirming the historical reality of the biblical narrative as well as God's divine intervention on behalf of the children of Israel, was the uncovering of the ancient city of Jericho.

You will recall that in Joshua 6, God informed Joshua that He had "given Jericho into your hand, with its king and the valiant warriors" (v. 2). The children of Israel were to march around the fortified city every day for six days, and then on the seventh day they were to march around the city seven times, with the priests blowing their trumpets on that seventh time.

Joshua 6:5 reads, "It shall be that when they make a long blast with the ram's horn, and when you hear the sound of the trumpet, all the people shall shout with a great shout; and the wall of the city will fall down flat, and the people will go up every man straight ahead." Note that the customary technique of using battering rams to knock down enemy walls was not employed here. Clearly, this was a supernatural event and likely a test of Israel's obedience and faith.

This same chapter tells us two other specific details regarding the ancient city of Jericho and this siege by the Israelites. First, in what was a rare architectural design in that time, dwelling places (apartments by today's standards) were built into the exterior walls of Jericho. Second, verse 24 informs us that Joshua and his army "burned the city with fire, and all that was in it."

In 1907, a German team of archaeologists led by Ernst Sellin and Carl Watzinger uncovered the ancient city of Jericho. What these men discovered shocked the secular world: The walls of Jericho had, in fact, fallen outward! Furthermore, the walls had fallen in a way that would have allowed, as verse 5 indicates, for "the people to go up every man straight ahead." This outward fall of the stone walls was and is unprecedented; no one has ever seen anything else like it. It is entirely inexplicable—outside of the supernatural explanation found in Joshua 6. And, as you might have guessed, remnants of little apartments built into the exterior walls were discovered, as well as evidence that the entire city was burned to the ground after the siege.

Reliable Transmission (and Early Composition)

It is widely acknowledged among experts in the study of ancient writings that the Hebrew scribes and priests were perhaps *the* most fastidious and serious guardians of their written texts and oral traditions. Each and every time the Pentateuch (writings of Moses), for example, was transcribed from one scroll to another, careful attention was paid in accounting for every syllable, every letter, and every mark of punctuation. Severe penalties were levied against the priest that missed even a single word! The Masoretic (Hebrew) text of the Old Testament, therefore, is considered to be one of the marvels of antiquity.

Dr. Robert D. Wilson wrote:

> That the original scribes should have written them with such close conformity to correct philological principles is a wonderful proof of their thorough care and scholarship; further, that the Hebrew text should have been transmitted by copyists through so many centuries is *a phenomenon unequaled in the history of literature* ... The proof that the copies of the original documents have been handed down with substantial correctness for more than 2,000 years cannot be denied. (Wilson, *A Scientific Investigation of the Old Testament*, 64, 85, italics mine)

F.F. Bruce adds:

> The Masoretes were well disciplined and treated the text with the greatest imaginable reverence, and devised a complicated system of safeguards against scribal slips. They counted, for example, the number of times each letter of the alphabet occurs in each book; they pointed out the middle letter of the Pentateuch and the middle letter of the whole Hebrew Bible, and made even more detailed calculations than these. (Bruce, *BP*, 117)

The only problem for Old Testament scholars was that the oldest existing Masoretic manuscript was the *Cairo Codex*, dating back to A.D. 895, which was a full 1,300 years after the very latest Old Testament writings. This was a major sticking point for skeptics of the Bible, especially in the areas of reliable transmission and early composition. I say *was* because all of that dramatically changed in 1947.

The Dead Sea Scrolls

In March of 1947, a Bedouin shepherd boy was searching for a lost goat among some caves along the western bank of the Dead Sea. He tossed a stone into one of the caves, hoping to startle the goat and send him running out of the cave. Well, the goat never emerged out of that cave, but what did emerge was nothing less than the most significant discovery of ancient manuscripts the world had ever seen—the Dead Sea Scrolls.

What are the Dead Sea Scrolls, and how are they relevant to our discussion here? The scrolls are made up of approximately 40,000 inscribed fragments that, when pieced back together again, form some 500 books. Many of the books reflect the culture and laws of the Essenes from the second century B.C. to first century A.D., writings such as the *Zadokite Documents* and the *Manual of Discipline*. (The Essenes were a strict Jewish sect that preserved and hid away the scrolls prior to the Roman invasion of Jerusalem in A.D. 70.) However, by far the most important subset of the Dead Sea Scrolls is the copies of the entire Old Testament, with the exception of the Book of Esther. The best preserved of all is, interestingly, the book of Isaiah, which was written on leather and not parchment. We'll come back to the Isaiah scroll in just a bit.

So how does this help us in assessing the reliability of the Old Testament text? In short, when the scrolls were discovered, we suddenly had manuscripts dated over a thousand years earlier than our oldest extant copies of the Masoretic text (*Cairo Codex*, etc.). We could simply compare the two side by side. This is precisely what scholars did, and what they discovered was that the texts were virtually identical!

World-renowned Bible scholar Gleason Archer had this to say, specifically about the Isaiah scroll:

> … even though the two copies of Isaiah discovered in Qumran Cave 1 near the Dead Sea in 1947 were a thousand years earlier than the oldest dated manuscript previously known (A.D. 980), they proved to be *word for word identical* with our standard Hebrew Bible in more than 95% of the text. The 5% of variation consisted chiefly of obvious slips of the pen and variations in spelling. They do not affect the message of revelation in the slightest. (Archer, *A Survey of Old Testament Introduction*, 23–35, italics mine)

Professor William Green, in his summation of the impact of the Dead Sea Scrolls wrote, "It may safely be said that no work of antiquity has been so accurately transmitted" (Green, *General Introduction to the Old Testament*, 81).

How, exactly, does this mountain of evidence square with Joseph Smith's indictment of the Bible, the notion that "ignorant translators, careless transcribers, or designing and corrupt priests have committed many errors"? It doesn't. And if we have documentary proof that the Hebrew text was essentially the same in B.C. 125 as it was in A.D. 895 as it is in present day, when exactly does Joseph Smith propose that these distortions took place? And who exactly is this pre-B.C. 125 "great and abominable church" that wreaked so much havoc on the Bible? Clearly it could not be the Roman Catholic Church, or any of the Christian sects, for that matter.

WHEN EXACTLY DOES JOSEPH SMITH PROPOSE THAT THESE DISTORTIONS TOOK PLACE?

One final thing before we conclude this chapter. Students of the Book of Mormon know that over a dozen chapters are lifted directly from Isaiah and nestled right into 2 Nephi. The actual texts, however, when compared head to head, differ quite significantly. These portions of Isaiah are alleged to have come from the brass plates of Laban, secured by Nephi himself prior to his family's escape from Jerusalem. Joseph Smith claimed that those portions of the Old Testament included in the Book of Mormon, including the writings of Isaiah, are essentially the *only* ancient Hebrew writings that could be fully trusted. Based on his understanding of the "corruption" of the Bible, this only makes sense. So, which version of Isaiah is correct? If they are different, they cannot both be right. The Dead Sea Scrolls, and specifically the supremely well-preserved Isaiah scroll, would settle this question once and for all.

BYU professor Lewis M. Rogers, after thoroughly inspecting the Isaiah scroll, wrote this in 1963:

> Latter-day Saints have cause to rejoice with other Christians and Jews for the new light and fresh perspective brought to them by the Dead Sea Scrolls, but occasionally they need to be reminded that their hopes and emotions make them vulnerable. It is quite possible that claims for the Book of Mormon and for LDS theology will not be greatly advanced as a consequence of this discovery.

(Saying that the discovery of the Dead Sea Scrolls may not advance the claims of the Book of Mormon or LDS theology could well have been the understatement of the year.)

Dr. Sidney Sperry, the most respected LDS expert of ancient writings in the 1960s, was somewhat blunter: "This tedious task [of analyzing the Isaiah scroll] has revealed that the scroll seldom agrees with the departures of the Book of Mormon text from that of the conventional Masoretic text of Isaiah. The Isaiah scroll is of relatively little use to Latter-day Saints as showing the antiquity of the text of Isaiah in the Book of Mormon" (BYU, 1963).

Of "relatively little use to Latter-day Saints," Dr. Sperry? Would it not be more accurate to say that the Isaiah scroll completely *invalidates* the departures found in the Book of Mormon? Is it not also fair to say that, once again, the accuracy and reliability of the Bible has been confirmed? Yes, a resounding yes!

As for the Isaiah scroll not advancing LDS theology, perhaps what Dr. Rogers had in mind was Isaiah 43:10, which reads in part: "Before Me there was no God formed, and there will be none after me." Can you, my LDS reader, begin to see why, in light of Joseph Smith's teaching on the eternal regression of gods, it is that either the Bible has this right or Joseph Smith does? Do you see that both cannot be true? I hope so. And I hope you make the right choice.

Conclusion

My hope is that the preceding has helped you see that the Bible *is* the Word of God and *has* been translated correctly. It is only when we plant our feet firmly on the true Word of God that we can move confidently into a deeper understanding of God's redemptive work through His Son, Jesus Christ. And it is to this work that I will dedicate the balance of this book.

SECTION III
THE DILEMMA

CHAPTER 5

I AM UNDONE

For all have sinned and fall short of the glory of God.
—Romans 3:23

Martin Luther once wrote, "The world is like a drunken peasant. If you lift him into the saddle on one side, he will fall off again on the other side." Most of us, including believers, tend to fall off the horse toward the side of either legalism (seeking God's approval through strict obedience and good works) or license (doing whatever we want, disregarding God's laws altogether). By the fall of 1998, nearly six years after my departure from the Mormon faith, I was the poster boy for both! I was the drunken peasant.

For over twenty years, I had played the part of the legalist, with Mormonism being my particular brand of legalism. I didn't drink or smoke. I paid tithe and fast offerings. I always did my home teaching, attended church every Sunday, wore my garments, and even went to the temple fairly often (although I never felt comfortable there). Outwardly, I was a good Latter-day Saint. Inwardly, I was mortified by my own awfulness. I was lustful, selfish, arrogant, prideful, judgmental, and uncompassionate. And that's really just the beginning of my sin issues. I could literally fill a page or more. I was profoundly conflicted—righteous on the outside (or at least trying to be) and filthy on the inside.

Six years later, there was a complete inversion. I was outwardly promiscuous, beyond any reasonable limit; addicted to money and material possessions; foul-mouthed; overtly arrogant and boastful; dishonest with myself and others (mainly to cover up the above); etc. And as if this weren't bad enough, I wasn't attending church, wasn't doing anything to serve anybody else, and wasn't praying or reading God's Word. I didn't even know where my Bible was! Yet inwardly, I missed God terribly. In a strange way, I missed His laws. I craved His wisdom and guidance and peace. I was utterly devoid of all three. In a word, I was *lost*.

One morning in November of 1998, I was shaving my face. I found myself staring into my own eyes, repulsed by what I saw. I had grown to hate the man I had become. I fell back onto the edge of the tub, buried my face in a towel, and wept. I didn't know yet who I would become, but I knew who I could no longer be. It was as if God came to me that morning and said, "Enough is enough." And I agreed.

Christians talk a lot about our sin nature. We talk a lot about it because the Bible talks a lot about it. In and of itself, however, our sin nature makes up only one half of what we'll call *the dilemma*. The dilemma is this: God is holy. He is pure, righteous, benevolent, and magnificent. For anyone to be in His presence, God requires that person must also be holy. But we are not holy. In fact, in many ways, we are the opposite of holy. And yet, we desire to live forever in the presence of God in His holy kingdom.

THE DILEMMA IS THIS: GOD IS HOLY.

BUT WE ARE NOT HOLY.

Now, to be sure, some people are far better at doing good things and not doing bad things. I would never argue that my next-door neighbor is as depraved and sinful as, say, the death-row inmate who's been convicted of raping and murdering multiple innocent women. Clearly, there are degrees of human goodness and evil. The problem is, on judgment day we won't be compared to one another. Our righteousness is not and will not be graded on a bell curve. We are held to the standard of *God's* righteousness; this is a high standard indeed.

Paul, in one verse, summarizes the dilemma perfectly: "For *all* have sinned and fall short of the glory of God" (Ro 3:23, italics mine). Interestingly, the Greek translation for the word *all* is … all. *All* of us have sinned, and continue to sin, falling far short of God's standard of holiness. What a bummer.

In a recent sermon, my pastor, Brad Young (no relation to Brigham), told a story that perfectly illustrates this dilemma and the chasm between God's holiness and our depravity. I've embellished it a little bit.

Two guys, Tom and Hal, take off on a fishing boat out of Long Beach Harbor to do some camping out on Catalina Island, about twenty-five miles off the Southern California coast. About four miles from the island, the boat strikes a sharp object floating in the ocean and is quickly filling with water. Tom, as it turns out, is an excellent swimmer; he played water polo in college. Hal can barely tread water. Neither has time to grab hold of a life jacket before the boat sinks.

Within minutes, seized by panic and without any ability to swim, Hal succumbs to the rough, cold waters and drowns right near where the boat sank. Tom, being the athletic swimmer he is, takes off with smooth, powerful strokes toward Catalina Island. He goes one mile, two miles, three miles, and has just under a mile to go. In fact, Tom can see the white, sandy beach awaiting him. The problem is, he's exhausted. Tom's muscles begin to cramp up; he can't take another stroke. And although he was close, really close to making it to the island, ultimately Tom drowns and sinks to the bottom of the Pacific.

The question is: What were Tom's final thoughts as his body drifted down into the deep waters? Was he thinking to himself, "Well, hey, at least I made it farther than Hal"? Of course not! The fact is, they both suffered the exact same fate. They both ended up at the bottom of the ocean.

This, then, is the dilemma. Some of us are excellent swimmers, some of us average, and some of us can't swim at all. The dilemma, the absolute dire and hopeless situation we find ourselves in is this: God isn't asking us to swim to Catalina. His glory is so magnificent, so radiant, so other-worldly in its brilliance that what He's asking us to do in order to even survive His presence is to swim to Japan from California! Yes, it is *that* impossible. And unless you see yourself in a situation as dire as sinking in the cold waters of the ocean, it is unlikely that you will grasp for and hang on to a life jacket to save you. As long as you perceive that you've "got this," you'll keep swimming. And you will, in due time, sink.

To Bible readers, this wide discrepancy between God and man should come as no surprise. No one, not even the greatest of the prophets, catches even a glimpse of God's glory without being totally blown away. Notice how no one ever draws near to God and says, "Hello, God. Nice to see you! Hey, don't be such a stranger." No, it doesn't happen that way. From Moses to Daniel to John, they all basically react the same way when God approaches—they fall flat on their faces.

Isaiah, *the* prophet of Israel in his time, learned this the hard way. He was going along, receiving revelations from God for the entire house of Israel, making bold prophecies about the future, and just generally being the spiritual giant that he was. But we read in Isaiah 6:1–5 of his encounter with God's resplendent glory:

> In the year of King Uzziah's death I saw the Lord sitting on a throne, lofty and exalted, with the train of His robe filling the temple. Seraphim stood above Him, each having six wings: with two he covered his face, and with two he covered his feet, and with two he flew. And one called out to another and said, "Holy, Holy, Holy, is the Lord of hosts, the whole earth is full of His glory." And the foundations of the thresholds trembled at the voice of him who called out, while the temple was filling with smoke. Then I said, "*Woe is me, for I am undone!* Because I am a man of unclean lips, and I live among a people of unclean lips." (italics mine)

Take note of Isaiah's reaction, his first reaction. Does he lift up his eyes to fully take in God's splendor? Does he immediately begin to praise God for all of His glory? No, he does not. His first thoughts appear to be, *Oh my goodness, I never had even the slightest clue of how resplendent God's glory really is. And now, by comparison, I realize that I am absolutely nothing! I am undone.*

Elsewhere, Isaiah sums up his people's attempt to please a holy God by writing, "For all of us have become like one who is unclean, and all our righteous deeds are like filthy rags" (Is 64:6). In the ancient Hebrew, "filthy rags" literally means used menstrual cloths. Not a very flattering picture, is it? And these were their *righteous* deeds?

I know that the concept of the utter sinfulness of man is very difficult for the Latter-day Saint to embrace. It goes against Mormon teaching with regard to both the fall of Adam and the fundamental nature of man. Let's take a brief look at each of these.

The Garden Conundrum

Joseph Smith taught that God gave Adam and Eve two conflicting commandments in the Garden of Eden:1) Multiply and replenish the earth. 2) Do not eat of the fruit of the Tree of Knowledge of Good and Evil, for if they did so, they would die. The conflict, for Latter-day Saints at least, is that unless they *did* eat of the fruit, they wouldn't be mortal/sexually capable and therefore would not be able to obey the first commandment to multiply and replenish the earth. Well, first of all, I don't see anywhere in Scripture where

God establishes conflicting, inter-negating laws and then requires man to somehow find his way out of the conundrum. It is not in God's nature to do so. Second, it is, in my opinion, an unwarranted extrapolation to assume that Adam and Eve were sexually innocent in their initial, paradisiacal state in the garden. The animals all seemed to be able to figure it out. Why couldn't Adam and Eve live, procreate, and prosper like the rest of the animal kingdom?

In any event, Lucifer came along and seduced Eve into disobeying God and partaking of the forbidden fruit. We all know what happened next. Adam and Eve were cast out of the garden and then subject to the common difficulties of life and, ultimately, to physical death. But here's where LDS theology deviates radically from biblical Christianity in relation to this issue of sin and sin nature.

LDS scripture and every prophet from Joseph Smith down has taught that the fall of Adam was essentially a good thing. It was not sin per se but rather a necessary part of God's overall plan. It is, in a sense, something to be celebrated, not lamented. Mormon theology also maintains that there is a fundamental disconnect between Adam and Eve's choice (of disobedience) in the garden and the basic nature of their posterity. Joseph Smith felt so strongly about this that he included it as the second of thirteen Articles of Faith: "We believe that men will be punished for their own sins, and not for Adam's transgression."

You'll get no argument from the Christian on this point; we are all accountable for our own choices in this life. However, what's missing here is the transmission, the conveyance if you will, of Adam's (and Eve's) willfully disobedient nature to his children, children's children, and so on to this present day.

Several LDS prophets and apostles have sought to downplay the seriousness of Adam and Eve's choice in the garden. Let's look at a sampling of these comments.

President Joseph Fielding Smith, in his book *Doctrines of Salvation*, wrote, "This was a transgression of the law, but not a sin in the strict sense, for it was something that Adam and Eve had to do!" (*DS*, 1:115). But what exactly is sin but a transgression of God's law? And if it was something they *had* to do, where was their free agency? Isn't agency a foundational principle of Mormon doctrine?

Marion G. Romney, an apostle at the time, said this at General Conference in April, 1953: "I do not look upon Adam's action as a sin. I think it was a deliberate act of free agency. He chose to do that which had to be done to further the purposes of God." Here Elder Romney seems to be doubling down on this utterly contradictory notion that Adam and Eve were simply exercising their free agency (in disobeying God), and yet it was something they *had* to do. And if they had to do it, were they free not to? It's not like there were several other couples God could have turned to in order to get the job done.

And finally, this quote from Sterling W. Sill of the Quorum of the Seventy: "Adam fell, but he fell in the right direction. He fell toward the goal. Adam fell, but he fell upward" (July, 1965). While this statement seems to defy both logic as well as gravity, it is a rather concise summation of the LDS view of the fall.

But what does the Bible say regarding the fall of Adam and the impact that event had on Adam's posterity? In Romans 5:12, Paul, speaking of Adam, says, "Therefore, just as through one man sin entered the world, and death through sin, and so death spread to all men, because all sinned ..." Paul then repeats the same point several more times in this chapter, so as to leave no room for doubt about what he means. Verse 18 says, "So then as through one transgression there resulted condemnation to all men, even so through one act of righteousness there resulted justification of life to all men."

The Default Setting

So, it is Christ to the rescue via His one act of righteousness. But this is a rescue from what? It is a rescue from the condemnation that spread to all men, every last one of us, through Adam's original sin. Our "default setting," then, as hard as it might be for the Latter-day Saint to accept, is condemnation. We are eternally condemned unless and until we are saved.

You ask, "Is this really what the Bible teaches?" Let's find out.

Paul, in his letter to the Ephesians, referring to all those living outside of God's grace (including their former selves) wrote, "Among them we too all formerly lived in the lusts of our flesh, indulging the desires of the flesh and of the mind, and were *by nature* children of wrath, even as the rest" (Eph 2:3, italics mine). We are *by nature* children of God's wrath. Why? Because we continually dishonor Him through our sinfulness; it's as simple as that.

John the Baptist weighs in with this: "Whoever believes in the Son has eternal life, but whosoever rejects the Son will not see life, for *God's wrath remains on him*" (Jn 3:36, italics mine). God's wrath *remains* on him? God's wrath upon sinful man is the normative setting? I just don't know about all this. Maybe Paul and John the Baptist were wrong. What did Jesus have to say on this issue? I'm glad you asked.

In His now famous late-night interview with Nicodemus, Jesus said, "He who believes in Him is not judged; he who does not believe has been *judged already*, because he has not believed in the name of the only begotten Son of God" (Jn 3:18, italics mine). Jesus is clearly teaching that our default setting, by virtue of being born "of the flesh," is judgment and condemnation. This is why He so emphatically stresses to Nicodemus the importance of being "born again" of the Spirit. Jesus said, "Truly, truly, I say to you, unless one is born again he cannot see the kingdom of God" (Jn 3:3).

We will discuss this subject of being born again much more later on, but for now, the important point Jesus is making is that it is not enough to simply be born into this world, born of flesh and blood. In fact, being born into this world assures you of exactly one thing: condemnation.

BEING BORN INTO THIS WORLD ASSURES YOU OF EXACTLY ONE THING: CONDEMNATION.

A Parenthetical Thought

There is a critical issue that I wish to address, and this seems to be the logical place to insert it. Forgive me the slight detour from our topic.

I find it more than ironic, in light of the above discussion, that Latter-day Saints often view evangelical Christians as taking the easy road, "easy grace" as it were. The perception on the part of most Mormons is that if all a person has to do is believe in Jesus to be saved and go to heaven, then what would ever motivate him or her to live a life of obedience to God? Wouldn't that just breed complacency in the life of the Christian?

But have you ever considered the full ramifications of Joseph Smith's teachings on the pre-mortal existence and the grand council in heaven? Remember, Joseph Smith taught (and the church still teaches) that essentially everyone born into this world, with the exception of murderers and sons of perdition (a rarity), is guaranteed entrance into the lowest of the kingdoms of heaven, the telestial kingdom. He taught that adulterers, whore mongers, liars, and the like—those who never do come to faith in Christ in this world or in spirit prison—still go to heaven. Furthermore, Joseph Smith was reported to have said that if we could just get one little glimpse of the telestial kingdom, we'd be tempted to take our own lives to get there. And Doctrine and Covenants (D&C) 76:89 says that the glory of the telestial "surpasses all understanding." Sounds like a pretty good place to me.

Now, why does the unbeliever still go to heaven—albeit to the lowest level? Because, according to LDS theology, the fact that you were born into this world and received a physical body is proof that you chose wisely in the pre-mortal world whom would be savior of this world. You chose Jehovah, the pre-mortal Jesus. Those that chose Lucifer were cast out of the heavenly realms and never were allowed to receive a body.

I call this the *retroactive efficacy of Christ's atonement*. You chose Christ as Savior before this world ever was. Therefore, in order to enter into the lowest level of glory, you never have to choose Him again. To the Christian, this doctrine not only appears to breed complacency, but also it is dangerous. You see, if a Mormon missionary and an evangelical Christian missionary were evangelizing a lying, whore mongering adulterer who refused to come to faith in Christ, who would feel the most urgency to bring this fellow to the truth? Clearly the Christian missionary, because if this man doesn't come to saving faith in Christ, he will suffer eternal anguish, separated from God forever, where there is "weeping and wailing and gnashing of teeth" (Mt 13:49–50). If the Mormon missionary fails to persuade this fellow, the very worst thing that will happen to him, according to LDS theology, is eternal separation from the Father but in a kingdom of glory that's still pretty comfortable—no weeping, wailing, or gnashing of teeth.

So, as it turns out, the most ironic twist in the whole Mormon-Christian theological debate is the fact that it is *Mormon* teachings that breed the most dangerous form of complacency, not the Christian concept of being saved by grace. Despite all the rigorous requirements to "prove yourself worthy to return to Heavenly Father" (that is, in the celestial kingdom), Mormons let everyone else off pretty easy.

Now, according to LDS scripture (D&C 19), the unrepentant sinner must suffer for his sins (even as Christ suffered) before he or she enters into the telestial kingdom. So that couldn't be a whole lot of fun. (This is sort of the Mormon version of purgatory.)But even this assumes that the suffering of any given sinner could appease the demands of justice of a holy God. The Bible is crystal clear that only the blood of the pure, unblemished lamb (Christ) can pay the price for our sin. We will discuss this much more in Chapter 8.

To my LDS reader who wonders why a Christian co-worker or classmate always seems to be against you, or at least against the doctrines of Mormonism, this is one of the doctrines that serves as a Christian's call to action. Can you begin to see why?

All of Us Like Sheep

And now back to our discussion of our sin nature. We've established that the Bible teaches, in broad terms, a universal, inescapable sin nature for all mankind. But certainly an individual who really tries hard can lift himself above the muck of humanity, right? Didn't Jesus challenge us to be "perfect, even as my Father in heaven is perfect" (Mt 5:48)? Certainly someone, at some point, was able to break free through his or her own righteousness, and not really need a savior, right? Let's see what some of our heroes of the Bible have to say about this.

David makes his assessment in these verses of a psalm: "God has looked down from heaven upon the sons of men to see if there is anyone who understands, who seeks after God. Every one of them has turned aside; together they have become corrupt; there is no one who does good, not even one" (Ps 53:2–3). And David would know, wouldn't he? For all the good he did eventually and for all the grace and forgiveness he received from God, David was guilty of some pretty awful stuff.

Three hundred years later, in one of the great messianic prophecies, Isaiah wrote this: "All of us like sheep have gone astray, each of us has turned to his own way; but the Lord has caused the iniquity to fall on Him" (Is 53:6). All of *us*, Isaiah says. Not all of *them*. And is this really so difficult to grasp? Is there anyone holding this book that can say that he or she has a good, solid handle on personal sin issues? Do you know of anyone who is essentially without sin? Do you know of anyone who knows someone without sin? No, no, and no. Case closed. Despite all our efforts to be pure and holy, we're just not. And we never will be … on this side of heaven.

Paul spills his heart out in Romans 7. Listen to his candid confession: "For we know that the law is spiritual, but I am of flesh, sold into bondage to sin. For what I am doing, I do not understand; for I am not practicing what I would like to do, but I am doing the very thing I hate … For I know that *nothing good dwells in me, that is, in my flesh* …" (Ro 7:15, 18, italics mine). This is *Paul* we're talking about here. He is the greatest missionary who ever lived! And this man was deep into his ministry at the time he wrote this; he had dedicated his entire life to serving God and preaching the gospel. And he said *nothing* good dwelled in him? What a sobering thought.

Notice that in verse 18, Paul points out that nothing good dwelled in his *flesh*. Why this distinction? Because the Bible teaches we are actually of dual nature: spirit and flesh. Nothing good lives in our flesh because our flesh is the product of a corrupt, fallen world. God Himself, however, breathes our spirit into us. Lots of good dwells there. Paul illustrates this duality in his letter to the Galatians: "But I say, walk by the Spirit, and you will not carry out the desire of the flesh. For the flesh sets its desire against the Spirit, and the Spirit against the flesh; for these are in opposition to one another …" (Gal 5:16, 17).

So we see that not only are we dual in nature, but also these two natures are sworn enemies! We are walking, talking contradictions, and according to Paul, we always will be. Nowhere does he indicate that this battle between the flesh and the spirit ever abates. Our duty, our obligation is to be "led by the Spirit" and not the flesh (v. 18). But again, I'm getting ahead of myself.

WE ARE WALKING, TALKING CONTRADICTIONS, AND ACCORDING TO PAUL, WE ALWAYS WILL BE.

Let's get back to our story of Hal and Tom and their life-threatening dilemma of capsizing four miles off the coast of Catalina. So far, we've talked about the universal sin nature of man that is inherited from Adam as a result of his disobedience to God in the garden. We've also looked at the grim reality that each of us, at one point or another, has to come to terms with the fact that we are sinful too. Yes, we may have some wonderful qualities, such as compassion toward others, a strong work ethic, and dependability when given a task to do. But ultimately, when we get honest with ourselves, we have to admit that we are sinners too. In our story of Hal and Tom, this sinfulness is represented by our inherent swimming capabilities, or lack thereof. When measured against the task of swimming four miles in cold, rough waters, both Hal and Tom came up short, terminally short.

So, what does the water represent? What are they swimming against? In a word, they are swimming against the *Law*—God's Law. Initially given to the children of Israel through Moses, the Law is essentially the dos and don'ts of life. Do good things. Don't do bad things.

What does the Bible have to say about the law? What was its purpose? And how well did it turn out for everyone? We'll look at that in Chapter 6.

CHAPTER 6

THE LAW

> And in His law he meditates day and night.
>
> —Psalm 1:2

The Bible tells us the Law was "added because of transgressions" (Gal 3:19). Because man has the innate, incurable tendency to rebel against God and live for his own passions and agendas, God saw fit to set certain parameters on man's behavior, both good and bad. In today's parlance, we would say that God was setting "healthy boundaries." Under the Mosaic Law, when His children obeyed, they were blessed. When they disobeyed, they were cursed.

Take a minute to read Deuteronomy 28, and you'll get a feel for the dynamic one might have experienced under the Law in ancient Israel. Verses 1 and 2 read, "Now it shall be, if you diligently obey the Lord your God, being careful to do all His commandments which I command you today, the Lord your God will set you high above all the nations of the earth. All these blessings will come upon you and overtake you if you obey the Lord your God …" God then proceeds to lay out all the really wonderful blessings that the obedient can expect to receive from His hand. In verse 6, for example, He says, "Blessed shall you be when you come in, and blessed shall you be when you go out." Well, that pretty much covers it.

Starting in verse 15, however, we get the other side of the coin: "But it shall come about, if you do not obey the Lord your God, to observe to do all His commandments and His statutes with which I charge you today, that all these curses will come upon you and overtake you ..." This is where it gets really ugly. Verse 16 hints at the inescapability of God's curse upon the disobedient. It says, "Cursed shall you be in the city, and cursed shall you be in the country." How about if I move to the suburbs? Nope, you're cursed there too!

The fact is that the Law never would have been necessary had man shown the ability to behave himself. But he never has and, apparently, never will. Ironically, the Law not only was set in place *because* of sin, it also makes us *aware* of sin.

Have you ever walked into a room with no intention but to pass through that room and on to another place? Ordinarily you would have no desire to touch your finger against the far wall of this room, would you? But then you see a sign taped to that wall that reads: "Wet paint. DO NOT TOUCH!" *Oh man. Now I've* got *to touch it, just to see if the paint's still wet.* Got to ... Sure enough, it's still tacky, and now you've left a smudge mark right where you touched.

Paul admitted his love for wet paint: "What shall we say then? Is the Law sin? May it never be! On the contrary, I would not have come to know sin except through the Law; for I would not have known about coveting if the Law had not said, 'YOU SHALL NOT COVET.' But sin, taking the opportunity through the commandment, produced in me coveting of every kind; for apart from the Law sin is dead" (Ro 7:7–8).

The Bible also teaches us that the Law was our custodian, our babysitter, if you will, until faith arrived. In Galatians 3:23–24 we read, "But before faith came, we were kept in custody under the law, being shut up to the faith which was later to be revealed. Therefore, the Law has become our tutor to lead us to Christ, so that we may be justified by faith."

I remember when I was young, I always had a nagging resentment of being forced to go to school. As I walked the five blocks to my elementary school, I saw adults watering their gardens or getting in their cars and driving away. Undoubtedly, they were heading off to work, but in my mind, they were free. No one told *them* what to do. Ironically, I was a very good student and earned my fair share of academic awards and recognition. But right on through high school, I hated that I was required by law to attend school.

Then in the fall of 1983, I packed my bags and headed off to college. Within a week, I realized this was going to be the hardest thing I'd ever do. I had to study Calculus, physics, biochemistry, and Shakespeare; write twenty-page term papers; take mid-terms; meet deadlines; and bear up under pressure I had never before experienced. But you know what? I loved it. Why? Because I was free. No one made me go to college; I chose to be there.

So, in my case, it was a good thing California law required me to go to school. Those requirements kept me in tow and forced me to learn the basic skills of reading, writing, and arithmetic until the time came when I *wanted* to engage in higher education. And so it is with God's laws.

Finally, the Bible teaches us that the Law is actually a curse to us. Paul spells this out plainly in Galatians 3:10: "For as many as are of the works of the Law are under a curse; for it is written, 'Cursed is everyone who does not abide by all things written in the book of the law, to perform them.'" Boy, talk about pressure. I am cursed if I do not abide by *all things* written in the book of the Law? I don't like my chances one bit if that's the standard. Paul would agree. In fact, he spares all of us the suspense in Galatians 2:16 when he writes, "… by the works of the Law no flesh will be justified."

The obvious question then is this: why would God establish His Law and require us to obey it, knowing full well that we would not be able to? Does He like setting us up for failure? Does He want to watch us struggle for the sake of struggling?

Jesus, in Matthew 5:20, seems to raise the bar to an absolutely unattainable level when He says, "For I say to you that unless your righteousness surpasses that of the scribes and Pharisees, you will not enter the kingdom of heaven."

So now He declares to the ordinary citizens of Jerusalem that they have to be more righteous than the spectacularly devout scribes and Pharisees? How can this be? No one was more obedient to God's law than those guys! And just when one of the men in the crowd thinks that maybe he can pull it off, Jesus delivers the knock-out punch: "You have heard that it was said, 'You shall not commit adultery'; but I say to you that everyone who looks at a woman with lust for her has already committed adultery with her in his heart" (Mt 5:27–28). Uh oh, who could possibly measure up to that standard? The answer is: no one. Remember, "For all have sinned and fall short of the glory of God."

So what is God's purpose in all this? Simply put, God has revealed to each of us that we are incapable of keeping His Law, not to make us feel bad but rather to make us feel desperate. As long as we think we can swim to shore, we will never cling to a life preserver to save us. The law convinces us of our desperate need for a Savior.

THE LAW CONVINCES US OF OUR DESPERATE NEED FOR A SAVIOR.

Mormons, in my experience, struggle with this. When I was LDS, I never viewed myself as weak, helpless, or desperate; quite the contrary. God had given me certain gifts and, along with will-power and determination, I was going to "prove my worthiness to return to live with Heavenly Father." Isn't that what we're here on earth to do? For me, having tangible things that I could check off my list—home teaching, tithing, word of wisdom, temple attendance—provided me with a sense of accomplishment and at least relative worthiness. Me, a hopeless sinner? No way. I had far too many things in my "good boy" box to ever raise suspicions, even to myself, that I was actually a vile sinner in desperate need of a Savior. Looking back now, LDS church meetings seemed more like swimming lessons to me than life preservation.

It is human nature to see in ourselves only what we want to see. And it is certainly in our religious nature to want to somehow prove to God, through an outward show of obedience and service, that we are worthy of His love and His blessings. Paul, in his letter to the Colossians, addresses this very issue:

> … why, as if you were living in the world, do you submit yourself to decrees, such as, "Do not handle, do not taste, do not touch!" (which all refer to things destined to perish with use)—in accordance with the commandments and teachings of men? These are matters which have, to be sure, the appearance of wisdom in self-made religion and self-abasement and severe treatment of the body, but are of no value against fleshly indulgence.
>
> —Colossians 2:20–23

How true, for me anyway. After all those years of not drinking or smoking; wearing my garments, even when it was 110 degrees outside; and not watching sports on Sunday, what exactly did that do for me? Was I any less sinful in my mind and heart? Nope, not one bit. But I did feel a whole lot less helpless and desperate.

In my research, I stumbled upon this quote by Joseph Fielding Smith, as recorded in *Doctrines of Salvation*: "Saints are the best people. We are, notwithstanding our weaknesses, the best people in the world … we are morally clean, in every way equal, and in many ways superior to any other people" (*DS*, vol I, p. 236).

Are Latter-day Saints the "best people in the world"? I really don't know. Maybe. The fact is, according to God's Word, the question is totally irrelevant. We *all* fall short. *None* is righteous, no not one. By the Law,*no* flesh is justified. Remember, in our story, Tom drowned too!

On second thought, maybe the question *is* relevant. Jesus, in His powerful parable of the Pharisee and the tax collector, as recorded in Luke 18:9–14, reveals the danger of thinking that you're a good swimmer (as well as the value of admitting that you're drowning). Take special note of Luke's preface to Jesus' parable:

> And He also told this parable to some people who trusted in themselves that they were righteous, and viewed others with contempt: "Two men went up into the temple to pray, one a Pharisee and the other a tax collector. The Pharisee stood and was praying this to himself: 'God, I thank You that I am not like other people: swindlers, unjust, adulterers, or even like this tax collector. I fast twice a week; I pay tithes of all that I get.' But the tax collector, standing some distance away, was even unwilling to lift up his eyes to heaven, but was beating his breast, saying, 'God, be merciful to me, the sinner!' I tell you, this man went to his house justified rather than the other; for everyone who exalts himself will be humbled, but he who humbles himself will be exalted."

This is a good time to ask yourself what kind of swimmer you are. Do you recognize the perils of the rough waters and immediately reach for the life preserver? Or do you swim yourself to the point of exhaustion, refusing to swallow your pride and grab hold of the one thing that will save you? I was definitely the latter. For close to forty years, I swam my heart out, thinking I really could make it to the shore. Finally, in 2004, I broke. I came to realize that I was never going to be good enough to please God or be worthy of His glory. I finally grabbed hold of the life preserver, and I haven't let go, not even for a minute. I was the Pharisee. Now, I am the tax collector. Which one do you most closely resemble?

Let me close this chapter with a passage from Romans that perfectly summarizes our dilemma and introduces us to the glorious solution:

> So then as through one transgression there resulted condemnation to all men, even so through one act of righteousness there resulted justification of life to all men. For as through the one man's disobedience the many were made sinners, even so through the obedience of the One the many will be made righteous.
>
> —Romans 5:18–19

It is my privilege now to tell you everything I know about the "obedience of the One."

SECTION IV
THE SOLUTION
(PART 1)

CHAPTER 7

WHO IS JESUS?

> For the Son of Man has come to seek, and to save that which was lost.
>
> —Luke 19:10

I still remember as if it were yesterday the first time I walked into a non-denominational Christian church after my six-year hiatus from religion. It was April, 1999, and I was head-over-heals in love with a girl who would eventually become my wife. She had invited me to her little church on Trask Avenue in Garden Grove called Calvary Chapel Westgrove. I wore a shirt and tie. Everyone else was in shorts and flip-flops.

The pastor, a handsome man in his late forties, rose to the pulpit and, with a broad smile, spoke these words: "We want to welcome everyone here this morning as we gather together to worship the Lord and celebrate His free gift of eternal life! Won't you please stand for our opening prayer?" (I know these words well because in my fourteen years at Westgrove, Pastor Brad rarely deviates from this opening salvo.)

Once the prayer was over, the music kicked in—a full band with electric guitar, drums, bass, and a group of singers! People remained on their feet, singing along and clapping their hands. It was the most unabashed, raw display of joy and exuberance I had ever seen—by a bunch of adults anyway.

And I remember thinking, *I'm sorry. What's happening here? What exactly are we celebrating?* It all seemed very juvenile to me that first Sunday and beneath me, in a sense. But I couldn't deny that these people were passionate about their worship. I had never seen anything like it. *Church is a celebration?* I was both amused and intrigued by what I experienced that day.

The one thing I could not get out of my mind was what Pastor Brad had said at the outset—that we were there to celebrate God's *free gift* of eternal life. *God's* free *gift of eternal life? How on earth could something as valuable as eternal life be free? Nothing else worth having is free. Plus, isn't it a bit premature to be celebrating? Wouldn't this sort of be counting our chickens before they hatch? We could still blow it.* Yet the confidence with which Brad had spoken it overwhelmed me and pierced my heart. I would never be the same.

And so finally, we get to the good stuff, the "good news" of the gospel: "For God so loved the world, that He gave His only begotten Son, that whoever believes in Him shall not perish, but have eternal life" (Jn 3:16). In this one solitary verse, Jesus lays out the entire gospel of salvation to Nicodemus and to all those who would ever read the Gospel of John. It is beautiful, eloquent, and simple.

Who Is Jesus?

Before we can consider the purpose and significance of Christ's sacrifice, we need to take a step back and identify Jesus for exactly who He is. Who is Jesus to the evangelical Christian, and how does this view differ from the view of the Latter-day Saint?

According to LDS theology, Jesus Christ was the firstborn spirit son of Elohim (God the Father) in the pre-mortal existence. Because we too are spirit children of God, this would make Jesus (Jehovah in the pre-mortal life) our elder brother. The key point here, though, is that Jesus was a created being just like the rest of us. He was selected by the Father to not only fulfill the role of Savior of the world (through His atoning sacrifice) but was also co-creator of the world (along with the Father and Michael, who would later become Adam). For my Christian reader, I apologize because I know this can be a little confusing.

According to LDS Apostle James Talmage, Jesus was subject to a "veil of forgetfulness," just like the rest of us, when he was born into this world (*Jesus the Christ*, p. 111). Over time, however, he grew "grace by grace" until he came to the full awareness of His role as Messiah, Savior of the world, God's mediator between Himself and sinful man. Through His death and miraculous resurrection, Jesus was elevated to His full, glorified status as God the Son, sitting at the right hand of God the Father. Mormons also believe Jesus will return to rule and reign on this earth during the thousand-year millennial era.

For the sake of time, I've decided not to delve into the LDS view of Christ's *ultimate* destiny, which would be to become a God (the Father) of His own world, populated with his own spirit children, borne to him by his many celestial wives. Suffice to say that, according to LDS theology, Jesus' ultimate destiny differs not one iota from that of the faithful, obedient Latter-day Saint man today.

I hope that by the end of this section, my LDS reader will begin to appreciate the dramatic difference between the Jesus of the Bible and the Jesus of Mormonism. The difference should not come as any great surprise, however. Remember, it was President Gordon B. Hinckley in an interview with Mike Wallace of *60 Minutes* who said this in June, 1998: "No, I don't believe in the traditional Christ. The traditional Christ of whom they speak is not the Christ of whom I speak. For the Christ of whom I speak has been revealed in this the Dispensation of the Fullness of Times."

This comment by President Hinckley, then, begs the question: who is the traditional Christ? Who does the Bible say that Jesus is? What are His origins, and what is His destiny? Let's find out.

The great Russian writer Fyodor Dostoyevsky, after his dramatic conversion from atheism to faith in Christ, once said that the Gospel of John was the only truly indispensable book on earth. He felt that the human race couldn't and wouldn't survive long without it. If this is true, one of the reasons for its lofty status might be in what we read in John's stunning introduction to his gospel: "In the beginning was the Word, and the Word was with God, and the Word was God" (Jn 1:1, 2). John leaves no room for doubt of whom he is referring when he identifies the *Word* in verse 14: "And the Word became flesh, and dwelt among us, and we saw His glory, glory of the only begotten from the Father, full of grace and truth." The Word was and is Jesus.

So, now, let's follow along as John reveals to us, step by step, the true nature of Jesus.

In the beginning was … Jesus. Before anything else existed, there was Jesus. He is self-existent, eternal, without beginning or end, the Alpha and the Omega. He is not, as Joseph Smith would have us believe, a created being. Rather, He is *Creator* of all things! (Interestingly, this is precisely what the Book of Mormon teaches in Alma 11:38–40.)

And Jesus was *with* God. This is another proof that Jesus was, and always has been, eternally co-existent with God. He is not the spirit product of God. He has always existed with God.

And Jesus *was* God. Can you imagine the reverberations that this statement would have caused among the skeptics of John's era? Can you even begin to imagine how John would have felt as this powerful truth gradually dawned on him? The God of this universe, Creator of heaven and earth and everything in it, asked John to take care of His mother in His absence! It takes my breath away.

Naturally, this leads us to the biblical definition of the triune nature of God, commonly referred to as the Trinity. God is one and yet manifests Himself as three distinct beings: the Father, the Son, and the Holy Spirit. Or, as explained in the New Bible Dictionary, "In the being of God there are not three individuals, but three personal self-distinctions within the one divine essence" (*NBD*, 2nd Edition, p. 1223).

In the Old Testament, God is sometimes referred to as *Elohim.* Joseph Smith claimed that Elohim is God the Father's name. In reality, Elohim is a title; it is not a proper name. In Hebrew, the title *Elohim* is singular, but it implies plurality. If you were to go scuba diving, for example, you might find yourself later describing to your friend a colorful, exotic school of fish that you encountered—one school, many fish. Elohim is like that. *Eloh*, in the Hebrew, means "God." The *im* denotes plurality. This is critically important to understand.

Jesus, then, is God the Son, the second manifestation of the triune God. He chose to come to earth and temporarily clothe Himself in human form in order to reconcile sinful mankind to Himself. Jesus is God incarnate.

Let's look closely at the Bible passages that teach this glorious truth, starting with the writer of Hebrews, who wastes no time in announcing the central theme of his epistle—the preeminent, divine nature of Jesus:

> God, after He spoke long ago to the fathers in the prophets in many portions and in many ways, in these last days has spoken to us in His Son, whom He appointed heir of all things, through whom also He made the world. And He is the radiance of His glory and the *exact representation of His nature*, and upholds all things by the word of His power.
>
> —Hebrews 1:1–3, italics mine

So, Jesus is not the Father. But He is the "exact representation" of the Father's nature. In John 14, we read a very fascinating conversation between Philip and Jesus. Jesus had just told His disciples that He is "the way, the truth, and the life; no one comes to the Father but through me."

Philip, in his limited understanding, made a simple request of Jesus: "Lord, show us the Father, and it is enough for us" (Jn 14:8).

Because Jesus was and is the exact representation of the Father, He was able to respond to Philip as follows: "Have I been so long with you, and yet you have not come to know me, Philip? He who has seen me has seen the Father; how can you say, 'Show us the Father'? Do you not believe that I am in the Father, and the Father is in me?" (Jn 14:9–10).

And we cannot find a more succinct description of the incarnate God, Jesus Christ, than in Colossians 1:15. It reads very simply: "He is the image of the invisible God …"

Invisible God? Joseph Smith taught that God (the Father) is a glorified, exalted man with a body of flesh and bone, the exact opposite of invisible. And Joseph Smith was unequivocally wrong. (Joseph Smith is also reported to have taught that the moon was populated by people who were, on average, six feet tall and dressed like Quakers! He was way off on that one too.)

Jesus, in his famous conversation with the woman at the well, told her, "God is spirit, and those that worship Him must worship in spirit and truth" (Jn 4:24).

John states very matter-of-factly in John 1:18, "No one has seen God at any time; the only begotten God who is in the bosom of the Father, He has explained Him." This resonates with Hebrews 1:3, doesn't it? Jesus *explains* the Father by simply being the "exact representation of His nature." John can declare this boldly because he learned it from a very reliable source. Jesus Himself proclaims, "Not that anyone has seen the Father, except the One who is from God; He has seen the Father" (Jn 6:46).

Yes, indeed. Jesus Christ, having eternally coexisted as God and with God outside the realm of space and time, has definitely seen the Father. He is intimately acquainted with the Holy Spirit as well.

This means that if Joseph Smith were telling the truth about seeing God the Father face-to-face in the grove that spring morning in 1820, he would have joined a very elite club indeed; for only Jesus Himself had ever seen the Father (see John 6:46 above). No one from Adam to Abraham to Moses to Jeremiah … right on down through James and John and Peter and Paul—none of them had seen or even *could* see the Father, because God is spirit. He is the invisible God. It is no coincidence that few hymns in the LDS hymnal are sung with more exuberance than "Praise to the Man." It is not, as most Christians would assume based on the title, a hymn of praise to Jesus Christ; rather it is a tribute to Joseph Smith.

I had a conversation recently with an LDS friend who reminded me of the more classic Mormon view of Jesus as God's representative sent to mankind. In other words, He was not *fully* God yet, at least, not during His mortal ministry. The Bible, however, clearly teaches that Jesus was fully God. Colossians 2:9 says, "For in Him all the fullness of Deity dwells in bodily form …" And in Colossians 1:19 we read, "For it was the Father's good pleasure for all the fullness to dwell in Him, and through Him to reconcile all things to Himself, having made peace through the blood of His cross …"

And finally, the most powerful attestation to God's incarnation in the man Jesus Christ is found in the New Testament: "… Christ Jesus, who, although He existed in the form of God, did not regard equality with God a thing to be grasped, but emptied Himself, taking the form of a bond-servant, and being made in the likeness of men. Being found in appearance as a man, He humbled Himself by becoming obedient to the point of death, even death on a cross" (Phil 2:5–8).

We learn several things from this fascinating passage. First, Jesus was actually God who took upon himself (temporarily) the form of a man. To an outsider, a non-believer, Jesus of Nazareth probably looked like a totally ordinary fellow. Isaiah prophesied that when Jesus arrived, he would have "no stately form or majesty that we should look upon Him, nor appearance that we should be attracted to Him" (Is 53:2).

Second, during His brief time on earth, Jesus willingly let go of His rightful "equality with God." The better translation for *grasped* here is actually *held on to* or *maintained.* When viewed in this light, it becomes clear that it's not as though Jesus had certain aspirations of *becoming* equal with God through His ministry and atoning sacrifice. No, He was and always has been God, but He chose to "empty Himself" for a season and take upon Himself the appearance of a man. Notice the verbiage: "in the *likeness* of men," "taking the *form* of a bond-servant," "found in *appearance* as a man." Get the picture? God incognito.

GET THE PICTURE?
GOD INCOGNITO.

You see, had Jesus appeared on the scene in His full, resplendent glory, everyone would have immediately bowed down and worshipped Him—Jews, Greeks, Romans, Assyrians, everyone. Not in a million years would they have rejected Him, let alone crucified Him! But Jesus wasn't seeking praise and worship … yet. That is not to say He didn't receive plenty of praise and adoration from His followers. Spectacular displays of His divinity and power radiated from Him continually. The miracles, the love, the compassion, the wisdom; no one had ever seen anything like this amazing Jesus of Nazareth. Yet His ministry, powerful and transcendent as it was, was not His primary objective.

Jesus said, "I am the good shepherd; the good shepherd lays down His life for the sheep" (Jn 10:11). *This* was His primary objective: to lay down His life for His sheep. And so we see the ultimate paradox: the shepherd *becomes* a lamb, a sacrificial lamb, in order to save His helpless but beloved sheep who have gone astray. What a beautiful picture.

THIS WAS HIS PRIMARY OBJECTIVE: TO LAY DOWN HIS LIFE FOR HIS SHEEP.

Could it have been any other way? Apparently not. Jesus says this to Nicodemus in their late-night meeting: "As Moses lifted up the serpent in the wilderness, even so must the Son of Man be lifted up; so that whoever believes will in Him have eternal life" (Jn 3:14–15, italics mine). Jesus said the Son of Man *must* be lifted up, but not in praise; quite the contrary. He was lifted up in shame and ridicule, beaten, spat upon, mocked, stripped down, and nailed to a cross in open humiliation. Irony of ironies: the most perfect, loving, moral man to ever walk this earth was treated as the most despicable and vile of offenders. God, Creator of heaven and earth, benevolent, omnipotent, holy God chooses to come to His world in order to teach, heal, and love on His creation—and we torture Him and nail Him to a cross.

And the most amazing thing of all is that Jesus would have it no other way. Hebrews 12:2 says, "Jesus, the author and perfecter of faith, who for the joy set before Him endured the cross …" *For the joy set before Him?* Yes, the joy of close, intimate fellowship with His children, in His kingdom, forever.

CHAPTER 8

THE CROSS

> For I determined to know nothing among you except Jesus Christ and him crucified.
>
> —1 Corinthians 2:2

And so here we are, friends, at the foot of the cross. Let's spend some time here. And let's not be in any rush. For this is where it all happened. This is where our souls were literally purchased by the precious blood of Jesus. This *is* our salvation. The cross of Jesus isn't part of the gospel; it *is* the gospel—and there is no other gospel! As Paul said, "For I determined to know nothing among you except Jesus Christ, and Him crucified" (1 Cor 2:2).

Looking back on my years in the Mormon church, I find it interesting that whenever the atonement was spoken of in sacrament meeting or Sunday school or even in General Conference, the speaker invariably said something like, "Brothers and sisters, for reasons we will never understand," or, "In a way that we will never comprehend," and then proceeded to discuss Christ bearing the sins of the world in the Garden of Gethsemane with maybe some mention of the cross—as if Christ's suffering on the cross were some incidental finishing touch on His sacrifice. But the emphasis was always on the mystery of the atonement, the incomprehensibility of Christ's sacrifice.

In reality, God has gone to great lengths to explain in tremendous detail the purpose of and need for the infinite gift of Christ on the cross, suffering and dying for all those who believe. The Bible makes it all absolutely crystal clear.

I admit that much of who God is and how He operates is a complete mystery. As God instructs Isaiah, "For as the heavens are higher than the earth, so are My ways higher than your ways and My thoughts than your thoughts" (Is 55:9). But as it concerns the finished work of our salvation, God leaves nothing to chance; He spells it out to us with perfect clarity.

Let's look at five foundational truths of Christ's atoning sacrifice.

God's Love

God is love. John tells us this in his first epistle (1 Jn 4:8). God is also light, power, holiness, and the prime mover in all of creation (and so much more). But His core, His very essence, is love. Everything He does and everything He creates flows from His all-encompassing love. And the most powerful demonstration of His love for all creation was His willingness to offer up His beloved Son to endure a horrible, painful punishment and death as payment for our sinfulness.

I am reluctant, having a son myself, to ask you who are parents to imagine the anguish of watching one of your precious children being viciously beaten and then nailed to a cross and left to die a slow, agonizing death. Isn't it amazing how quickly we block that image from our minds? Difficult as it is to play through that scenario, I believe it is a worthwhile exercise.

Could you hand over your little, six-year-old child to endure such brutal torture and death if it, for example, allowed ten vile criminals to be released from prison to start a new life? How about a hundred? Would you trade the life of your child for *any* number of bad guys? It's doubtful.

Now, let's turn this around. A bad guy forces himself into your house and demands the life of either you or your child. Would you even hesitate, Mom or Dad? Of course not. You would rush to lay your life down so that your child could live. Why? Love, pure and simple; we love our children more than ourselves. Ah, now we're getting somewhere. This very principle is *the* central theme of the entire gospel.

First John 4:8–10 states, "… God is love. By this the love of God was manifested in us, that God has sent His only begotten Son into the world so that we might live through Him. In this is love, not that we loved God, but that He loved us and sent His Son to be the propitiation for our sins." As wonderful and hope-filled as this passage is, it also reveals something that is both sad and ironic: "… not that we loved God, but that He loved us." So here we have this magnificent God who is at His very core loving, gracious, patient, generous, and kind. And despite all this, we (mankind) just don't love Him. We don't. It's hard to believe, isn't it?

Years ago, we had an early-morning seminary teacher named Sister Atwood. I wasn't of seminary age yet, but I remember my sister telling me that, despite Sister Atwood's best efforts, the kids continually rebelled against her and made her life pretty miserable. One day, in an effort to win the kids over, Sister Atwood baked a couple dozen cupcakes and carefully decorated them for each of her students. As she handed them out, she expressed her love and appreciation to each one of the kids. You want to know what those kids did with the cupcakes? They went directly out to the parking lot and smeared them all over Sister Atwood's car. That's astonishing cruelty, and very much within the parameters of human behavior.

The fact is, we love ourselves and are constantly seeking to meet our own needs and pursue our own agendas. When you think about it, are we really a whole lot different than the toddler going through the "terrible twos"? Not really. And yet, just as we unconditionally love our little toddlers, God loves us.

However, God's overwhelming love for us does not negate the fact that we are, by nature, enemies of God! I understand that most of my LDS readers will likely bristle at this judgment. "Me? An enemy of God?" It's far more comfortable to consider ourselves already in the good graces of God, spirit children born into His eternal family long before we ever came to this earth. However, this is a unique doctrine taught only by Joseph Smith. It is not at all supported by the Bible (despite the unique Mormon interpretation of Jeremiah 1:5).

What the Bible teaches, if you recall from Chapter 5, is that we are under condemnation, because of our sin nature, unless and until we come into saving faith in Christ. Paul puts it this way: "But God demonstrates His own love toward us, in that while we were yet sinners, Christ died for us" (Ro 5:8).

In other words, God didn't say, "Okay you lousy, no-good rebels. Clean up your acts, and then once I see some good, consistent effort on your part, then I will consider offering up a sacrifice on your behalf to save you. Otherwise, no dice." No. God demonstrated His love *first*. And it is long before we are actually deserving of such love.

The Book of Mormon teaches the exact opposite. In fact, it is in the stark contrast of this and many other doctrines found in the two books that forced me to admit to myself that the Bible and the Book of Mormon could not possibly both be true.

For example, Moroni admonishes us as part of his benediction: "Yea, come unto Christ, and be perfected in him, and deny yourselves of all ungodliness; and *if* ye shall deny yourselves of all ungodliness ... *then* is his grace sufficient for you ... through the shedding of the blood of Christ" (Moroni 10:32–33, italics mine).

See the difference? This, my dear Latter-day Saint friends, is *another gospel.* Moroni says I must first deny myself of "all ungodliness," and if I can do that, then and only then will God's grace cover me through the shedding of Christ's blood. This is a classic "if-then" proposition and a far cry from "while we were yet sinners."

If I could sit down with Moroni for a few minutes, I would ask him two questions. First, who among us has ever, will ever, or could ever deny himself of all ungodliness? Wouldn't the denial of all ungodliness be the equivalent of moral perfection? If all that's left is godliness, then couldn't we basically put a bow on it and call it good? Is this at all realistic, and if so, in whose world? Not in Paul's world, where we "all have sinned and fall short of the glory of God."

My second question would be: If I, through some Herculean effort, were somehow able to deny myself of all ungodliness, what exactly would I need God's grace for? Extra credit? Of which sins exactly would Christ's blood be cleansing me? It makes no sense.

I ran into a couple of Mormon missionaries recently who insisted that the church absolutely teaches that we are saved by grace. I borrowed their scriptures and opened to Moroni 10, asking them to explain to me the obvious discrepancy. One of them offered that this was "old times" (A.D. 421 to be exact) and that we now have modern prophets who teach that we are saved by grace.

I wonder if Spencer W. Kimball would be considered modern enough for these two sincere young men? In his classic *Miracle of Forgiveness*, President Kimball wrote, "Eternal life hangs in the balance awaiting the works of men. Living all the commandments guarantees total forgiveness of sins and assures one of exaltation ... Perfection, therefore, is an achievable goal" (*MoF*, p. 208).

PERFECTION, THEREFORE, IS AN ACHIEVABLE GOAL" (MOF, P. 208).

Seeking to become more and more Christ-like over the course of our lives is indeed a worthy endeavor and should be the core commitment of every true Christian. We should sin less and less as we are being sanctified over time by God's indwelling Holy Spirit. However, with all due respect to President Kimball, moral perfection is *not* an achievable goal. The Bible says, "If we say that we have no sin, we are deceiving ourselves and the truth is not in us" (1 Jn 1:8). It is best to admit that we are sinners saved by grace.

Getting back to Paul's writings, are we really *enemies* of God? Must we paint ourselves as being so antagonistic? I'm afraid so. Paul continues, "For if while we were *enemies* we were reconciled to God through the death of His Son, much more, having been reconciled, we shall be saved by His life" (Ro 5:10, italics mine).

So, here is what we can conclude: we are rebellious, selfish, and sinful creatures. We are natural-born enemies of God, and yet His love overwhelms our animosity. Jesus, in His famous Sermon on the Mount, taught this radical new standard: "... love your enemies ... so that you may be sons of your Father who is in heaven" (Mt 5:44). He could teach this because He learned it from His Father! And within a few short years of this very sermon, Jesus provided the ultimate demonstration of this love for one's enemies in dramatic fashion—at the cross of Calvary.

A Pure and Unblemished Offering

Both Christian and Latter-day Saint would agree that Jesus Christ lived a perfect, sinless life. Of the two, however, the Mormon is much more likely to see Christ's perfectly moral life as being primarily an example or standard set for us to strive for. And while the Christian certainly desires to become, over time, more and more like Christ, he is much less likely to view Christ's perfect life as *primarily* serving the purpose of being the gold standard. Rather, His perfect life qualified Him to be God's spotless, unblemished sacrificial Lamb. Jesus was the Lamb of God.

Without going into a lengthy discussion of the law of sacrifice carried out by faithful Jews under the Mosaic Law, students of the Old Testament recognize there was a daily ritual of sacrificing innocent, unblemished lambs and goats to atone for or cover the sins of the people. Furthermore, once a year, on the Day of Atonement (see Lev. 16), the High Priest would enter into the Holy of Holies and sprinkle the blood of an unblemished, firstborn male goat(that was sacrificed) on the mercy seat of God. But first, he would have to sacrifice a bull to purify himself, just to be able to enter into the Holy of Holies (the bull's blood was sprinkled on the mercy seat too). Meanwhile, there was a male goat standing at the ready outside the temple, waiting for his role in this annual ritual. We read in Leviticus 16:21–22:

> Then Aaron shall lay both of his hands on the head of the live goat, and confess over it all the iniquities of the sons of Israel and all their transgressions in regard to all their sins; and he shall lay them on the head of the goat and send it away into the wilderness by the hand of a man who stands in readiness. The goat shall bear on itself all the iniquities to a solitary land; and he shall release the goat in the wilderness.

Time and again, the Old Testament provides picture illustrations of New Testament truths. None is more clear than the image of Israel's sins being transferred onto an innocent, unblemished animal. One is sacrificed to atone for sin. The other is set free, allowing for the disposal of those sins out into the wilderness.

Christ, of course, put an end to the need for animal sacrifice once and for all. In an act totally lost upon the temple priests of His day, Christ was both High Priest *and* sacrificial lamb! The writer of Hebrews explains it this way:

> For Christ did not enter a holy place made with hands, a mere copy of the true one, but into heaven itself, now to appear in the presence of God for us; nor was it that He would offer Himself often, as the high priest enters the holy place year by year with the blood that is not his own. Otherwise, He would have needed to suffer often since the foundation of the world; but now once at the consummation of the ages He has been manifested to put away sin by the sacrifice of Himself.
>
> —Hebrews 9:24–26

In this same chapter we read, "For if the blood of goats and bulls … sanctifies for the cleansing of the flesh, how much more will the blood of Christ, who through the eternal Spirit offered Himself without blemish to God, cleanse your conscience from dead works to serve the living God?" (v. 13)

And so we see that Jesus Christ is the only one who could ever be a worthy sacrifice for sin because He is the only sinless, unblemished man. He and He alone qualifies to make atonement for sin because He is the only person ever born into this world who was not tarnished by this world. Hebrews 4:15 says, "For we do not have a high priest who cannot sympathize with our weaknesses, but One who has been tempted in all things as we are, yet without sin." The world couldn't tarnish Him. Then again, the world had no idea who it was dealing with.

Substitutionary Sacrifice

A closely related and equally important concept to grasp is the substitutionary nature of Christ's sacrifice. Looking back now, we clearly see that the slaughtering of innocent animals in the temple was merely a type, a symbol, of the last great sacrifice to be carried out by Christ Himself. Whether the people knew it or not, the blood of lambs didn't *actually* cleanse the consciences of the children of Israel. It was symbolic, a foreshadowing of what was to come.

God also instituted the law of blood sacrifice in order to impress upon the minds of His children His utter hatred for and intolerance of sin. It was meant to be gruesome. It was meant to be bloody. God hates sin *this* much!

Despite their best efforts, Israel continued to sin. (Yes, the Law was and still is that difficult to obey.)And so the blood of lambs continued to pour down the steps of the temple in Jerusalem—day after day, year after year. What an awful situation.

Paul writes, "For as many as are of the works of the Law are under a curse; for it is written, 'Cursed is everyone who does not abide by all things written in the Book of the Law, to perform them'" (Gal 3:10). So, the Law is a curse? No, our inability to abide by all things written in the Book of the Law is the curse. But remember, God didn't institute the Law in order to discourage us or make us feel bad. He laid out a stringent set of laws in order to make us feel *desperate*—desperate for a Savior. And this, of course, is where Jesus comes in.

Paul continues, "Christ redeemed us from the curse of the Law, having become a curse for us—for it is written, 'Cursed is everyone who hangs on a tree'" (Gal 3:13). Christ *became* a curse for us the day He hung on the cross at Calvary. Or as Paul says in 2 Corinthians 5:21, "He [God] made Him [Jesus] who knew no sin to *be sin* on our behalf …" (italics mine). So, Christ didn't just take our sin upon Him and pay for it on the cross; although, He certainly did do that. He also figuratively *became* sin on our behalf. Christ became sinful? No, not sinful. As He hung on the cross, writhing in indescribable pain, He *represented* sin—just like the innocent lambs of ancient Israel. How amazing is this? How wonderful is this Savior of ours?

Isaiah prophesied about this substitutionary sacrifice over 700 years before it happened. If there was ever any question about God's ability to reveal future events to prophets, Isaiah 53 removes all doubt. Here we read, "All of us like sheep have gone astray, each of us has turned our own way; but the Lord has caused the iniquity of us all to fall on Him…. But the Lord was pleased to crush Him, putting Him to grief; if He would render Himself as a guilt offering" (Is 53:6, 10). And render Himself Jesus did.

Okay, so sin was paid for vicariously by Christ suffering and dying on the cross. What about the Law? Did the Law survive the cross? Because if it did, I personally would feel very vulnerable going forward. And in light of my vulnerability, it's probably no coincidence that the answer to this question is my favorite passage of the entire Bible. Paul writes, "When you were dead in your sins and in the uncircumcision of your sinful nature, God made you alive with Christ. He forgave us all our sins, having canceled the written code, with its regulations, that was against us and that stood opposed to us; he took it away, nailing it to the cross" (Col 2:13–14, NIV).

I love this picture. Jesus Christ, God in the flesh, the one and only worthy Lamb, through His sacrifice, canceled the written code (the Law) by nailing it to the cross. I imagine the Law written on thin parchment, all of the rules and regulations carefully lined up in columns and in very fine print. I imagine the Roman soldiers as they are just about to drive thick nails through His hands. But before they do, Jesus carefully lays the parchment between the nails and His flesh. And as the blood generously flows from His wounds, it thoroughly saturates the parchment, covering over every single word written thereon. Technically, the Law is still there, but it is completely obscured by the crimson blood of Christ.

TECHNICALLY, THE LAW IS STILL THERE, BUT IT IS COMPLETELY OBSCURED BY THE CRIMSON BLOOD OF CHRIST.

To this day, I get emotional when I read this verse. I quoted this passage from the NIV because page 1566 of my old NIV Bible is still wrinkled and tear-stained from the very first time I read through the New Testament without the filter of religion. Certain moments in our spiritual rebirth can never be forgotten.

Do you find yourself being moved to tears when you contemplate Jesus suffering on the cross? Do you find yourself wanting to jump for joy as you accept the fact that because of His suffering, the law no longer condemns you? Maybe it takes a naturally arrogant, lustful, rebellious wretch like me to fully appreciate the promise of Colossians 2. Maybe the ultra "goody good" isn't particularly moved by this. I'll never know.

It is funny, though, how none of the pages of my old Book of Mormon are stained with tears. And certainly no part of my *Doctrine & Covenants* or *Pearl of Great Price* is. But now, every day of my life I find myself crying out, "Thank you, thank you, thank you, Jesus, for taking my place on the cross."

Propitiation

The word *propitiation* found in the New Testament is the English translation for the Greek word *hilasterion*, which means "to appease the wrath of." There can be no discussion of propitiation, therefore, apart from the backdrop of wrath—in this case, God's wrath for sin.

Both the Old and New Testaments are crystal clear about the wrath of God. God is holy, and as such, He cannot tolerate even the slightest degree of sin. To do so would be to undermine His purity and holiness—who He is. God hates sin and, of necessity, must punish it. There are no exceptions.

Now, the Bible also makes it clear that God is patient and "slow to anger." The unrepentant, however, is not to mistake God's patience for exoneration. Moses makes this very point with the ever-rebellious Israelites: "The Lord is slow to anger and abundant in loving kindness, forgiving iniquity and transgression; but He will by no means clear the guilty" (Num 14:18).

Paul seems to skip the "loving kindness" talk altogether when he writes, "For the wrath of God is revealed from heaven against all ungodliness and unrighteousness of men who suppress the truth in unrighteousness ..." (Ro 1:18).

There is a natural tendency for "good people," Latter-day Saint and Christian alike, to read a passage like this and think to themselves, *Boy oh boy. I sure am glad I'm not one of the ungodly or unrighteous!* But as we established in the previous section, we *are* all ungodly. We continually fall short of God's glory. Our very best attempt at righteousness is but "filthy rags." Any sort of honest moral inventory of ourselves reveals that we are not only unable to "prove our worthiness to return to Heavenly Father" but also that we are, in fact, invoking His wrath! Gee, I just can't win for losing. That is correct; *you* can't. But Jesus can, and He did.

The bad news/good news message is spelled out clearly in Paul's letter to the Romans:

"For all have sinned and fall short of the glory of God [bad news], being justified as a gift by His grace through the redemption which is in Christ Jesus [good news]; whom God displayed publicly as a *propitiation* in His blood through faith" (Ro 3:23–25, italics mine).

The editors of the *New Bible Dictionary* put it this way: "Propitiation properly signifies the removal of wrath by the offering of a gift." And so in simplest terms, when God says He displayed Christ "publicly as a propitiation in His blood through faith," it's like He's saying:

Dear Sinner,

I am a holy God who must punish sin. But my love for you exceeds my need to punish your sinfulness. Therefore, I have provided a way, through the sacrifice of my beloved Son, to appease my wrath. Jesus will drink the full cup of my wrath, draining it right down to the dregs. He will do this on your behalf. If (and this is where it all hinges for you), *if* you will receive this gift that I offer in faith, believing that I will keep my word, I will promise to no longer feel wrath towards you because of your sin.

This is my one and only offer. There is no other offer. And oh, by the way, this really is a no-brainer. Take the gift.

Love you always,
God

"Tetelestai"

In the Gospel of John, we read of the final moments of Jesus' life as He hung exhausted and dehydrated on the cross, clinging to literally His last few breaths, the last few beats of His heart. But He wasn't quite done yet. He had one final proclamation to make. Apparently, His mouth was so dry that He struggled to speak. Directing His attention to the nearby Roman soldiers, He very simply said, "I thirst."

Let's pick up these final moments in John 19:29–30: "A jar full of sour wine was standing there; so they put a sponge full of the sour wine upon a branch of hyssop and brought it up to His mouth. Therefore when Jesus had received the sour wine, He said, '*It is finished!*' And He bowed His head and gave up His spirit" (italics mine).

It is finished. That's such a simple phrase. Of all the things Jesus could have said as a farewell to this lost and corrupt world, why would He say, "It is finished"? He didn't give a grand speech to explain all that He had just done (remember, even His own disciples were unclear as to His date with the cross). There were no final words of advice on how we should live our lives. And there was no reminder about His own prophecy that in three days He would rise again. He just said, "It is finished," a fairly straightforward statement of the increasingly obvious. Or was it?

The phrase "It is finished" is the English translation for one word found in the original Greek text: *tetelestai*. This is one word with a profound meaning.

In Jesus' day, when a criminal was incarcerated, a list of his crimes was placed above the door of his cell, along with the length of his sentence. For example, the sign might read, "Here imprisoned is Benjamin of Jericho, guilty of theft and public violence, 20 years." Upon completion of the first year of his sentence, the sign would be changed to read "19 years," then "18," and on it went until the sentence was carried out to completion.

When the twenty-year sentence was up and Benjamin was set free from the cell, the entire sign would be removed and replaced with a placard that read simply, "Tetelestai," which in the Greek means "Paid in full." Benjamin's debt to society for the evil he had done was paid in full. The prisoner was set free.

And so we see that Jesus' final announcement to the world, to every person who had ever lived or would ever live, was that He had paid the price for every sin ever committed. This was no down payment; the full demands of God's justice had been thoroughly satisfied. The price for sin had been paid in full! And when something has been paid for in full, the balance is zero.

Peter writes in his first general epistle: "Knowing that you were not redeemed [paid for] with perishable things like silver or gold from your futile way of life inherited from your forefathers, but with precious blood, as of a lamb unblemished and spotless, the blood of Christ" (1 Pt 1:18–19).

It took me nearly forty years to understand why it is that church, for Christians who have been born again of God's Spirit, is a celebration. It finally made perfect sense to me that these people would clap and raise their hands and often weep openly (in church!) when they sang praises to their Savior. Now I do it too. I can't not do it. It wells up within me because I finally see Jesus' shed blood on the cross as payment in full for my sin! My salvation was purchased on that day, in that moment, by Jesus' incomparable, precious blood.

CHAPTER 9

THE SUFFICIENCY OF THE BLOOD

> In Him we have redemption through His blood.
>
> —Ephesians 1:7

Religion seeks, through rules, regulations, ordinances, and guidelines, all sorts of add-ons to supplement Christ's sacrifice on the cross. "Religionists" are guilty of treating the blood of Jesus as insufficient, as not having paid the price in full, or else why would they insist on adding to it?

My friend Shawn McCraney said it best in his fantastic book *I Was a Born-Again Mormon*:

> Because God offered His Only Begotten Son as the supreme sacrifice for the world, and because the Son willingly gave Himself over to all the misery and suffering incurred from God's perfectly just wrath, no offering could ever take His place; no other deed, sacrifice, payment, or attempt at worthiness will gain acceptance from Almighty God other than the righteous and complete payment of His Son. There is no act, deed, amount of money, service, work, diligence, ordinance, attendance, temple rite, testimony, or self-sacrificial offering of any kind that could ever take any part of restoring fallen humanity to the presence of God. I cannot emphasize this point too emphatically. Such faithless acts or attitudes

> aren't needed, aren't worthy, and would never meet the demands of perfect justice that God demands for sin and rebellion. Few human ideologies more readily mock God, religious or otherwise, than for human beings to think they could ever do anything to contribute to the suffering, sacrifice, payment or atonement for sin Jesus gave on the cross. And yet it happens all the time.
>
> —McCraney, *IWBAM*, p. 30

Are you ever guilty of "Jesus plus"? Is your salvation a combination of what Jesus did for you on the cross, *plus* your efforts to please God (i.e., baptism, tithing, doing good unto others, etc.)? If so, it's Jesus plus. And if it's Jesus plus, then essentially what you're insisting is that His final declaration was, "Paid in part." I don't know how to say that in Greek, but I know it's not *tetelestai*.

Recently I had a rather animated debate with an LDS friend over this issue of the sufficiency of Christ's redeeming blood. My point to him was that the Bible was unambiguous about two key doctrines: 1) We are saved by the grace of God through faith alone, in Christ alone. 2) The blood of Christ shed on the cross is entirely sufficient to pay the price for any and all sins committed by anyone at any time. No one and no sin is outside the cleansing, redeeming power of His blood. To my surprise, he agreed. He then went on to claim that this was precisely what the LDS church teaches and has always taught. This, I informed him, is categorically untrue.

In his book *Miracle of Forgiveness*, Spencer W. Kimball, twelfth president of the LDS church, wrote, "One of the most fallacious doctrines originated by Satan and propounded by man is that man is saved alone by the grace of God; that belief in Jesus Christ alone is all that is needed for salvation" (*MoF*, p. 206). So, in relation to my first point, I pointed out that a fairly recent LDS prophet taught that not only is faith in Christ not sufficient to save us but also that this "fallacy" was, in fact, concocted by Satan to lead people astray. Once again, a central teaching of the Bible is reclassified by the Latter-day Saints as an instrument and doctrine of Satan.

Regarding my second point, about the sufficiency of Christ's atoning blood, I reminded my friend of the LDS teaching that there is no forgiveness for murder (murder being sufficiently egregious as to be outside the reach of Jesus' sacrifice) and also of the era in church history in which the doctrine of "blood atonement" was taught and practiced.

Most Mormons today are uninformed about the doctrine of blood atonement, but they shouldn't be; it was taught and expounded upon by numerous LDS prophets and apostles spanning over a hundred years. Those who understand the doctrine tend to deny it altogether or consider it to be slanderous, anti-Mormon propaganda. You'll see why presently.

The tenth president of the LDS church, Joseph Fielding Smith, wrote the following under the heading "True Doctrine of Blood Atonement" in his popular book *Doctrines of Salvation*:

> Just a word or two now on the subject of blood atonement. What is the doctrine? It is simply this: Through the atonement of Christ, all mankind may be saved, by obedience to the laws and ordinances of the gospel. But man may commit certain grievous sins—according to his light and knowledge—that will place him beyond the reach of the atoning blood of Christ … If these offenses are committed, then the blood of Christ will not cleanse them from their sins even though they repent … If then he would be saved *he must make sacrifice of his own life* to atone for that sin, *for the blood of Christ alone under certain circumstances will not avail …*
>
> —*DoS,* pp. 133–136, italics mine

This from the prophet of God's "one true church" on earth: the blood of Christ, in the case of certain serious sins, is unable to atone for those sins, but the sinner's blood is. Could there be a less Christian doctrine than this? It would be hard to think of one.

Was this an isolated teaching found only in Smith's *Doctrines of Salvation*? Hardly. Elder Bruce R. McConkie, who ironically denied that the doctrine of blood atonement was ever taught or practiced in the early days of the church, nevertheless confirmed that it is a true doctrine in his classic *Mormon Doctrine*: "… under certain circumstances there are some serious sins for which the cleansing of Christ does not operate, and the law of God is that men must have their own blood shed to atone for their sins" (*MD*, 1958 edition, p. 87).

I could have sworn that Christ "forgave us *all* our sins" and that He took away the written code, "nailing it to the cross" (Col 2:13–14). Elder McConkie says otherwise. He insists that in the really tricky cases, Jesus' blood falls short; whereas our blood comes through wonderfully. According to this way of thinking, the blood of the murderer is a worthy offering of atonement, but the blood of God's precious, perfect Son is not. How offensive. How utterly sickening to the Christian heart.

Where did this doctrine come from? It was originally taught by early church leaders in Nauvoo, Illinois; although, not openly. It wasn't until 1856 that second church president Brigham Young taught it openly from the pulpit in the tabernacle. It was in General Conference that year that Brigham Young laid out this chilling scenario:

> Let me suppose a case. Suppose you found your brother in bed with your wife, and put a javelin through both of them, you would be justified, and they would atone for their sins, and be received into the kingdom of God. I have no wife whom I love so well that I would not put a javelin through her heart, and I would do so with clean hands … There is not a man or woman who violates the covenants made with their God that will not be required to pay the debt. *The blood of Christ will never wipe that out, your own blood must atone for it.*
>
> —*Journal of Discourses*, Vol. 3, p. 247

I invited my friend to e-mail me his rebuttal regarding these teachings. That was over three months ago. Still no word …

Perhaps some of my LDS readers are feeling right about now that I've broken my promise that this book would not be a prosecution of Mormonism. I can understand why you might feel this way. But some teachings are so serious that they must be exposed, evaluated on their merits, and dealt with accordingly. I cannot stand by and allow for a doctrine that devalues the blood of Jesus and then assigns value (*any* value, let alone atoning value) to the blood of a sinner. I'm asking you, my LDS reader, to give serious consideration to this unique doctrine of blood atonement and ask yourself if you can, in good conscience, belong to a church that teaches it or has ever taught it. Please see it for what it clearly is: a dangerous rejection of the sufficiency of the cross.

This very concept of God's completed work of redemption through the cross of Jesus is *the* single most important truth discussed in this entire book. Every single word I've written up to this point has been a preparation for this very moment, and everything I'll write going forward only further explains this glorious, eternal, life-saving truth: Christ on the cross, dying for our sins, *is* our salvation. This *is* the good news of the gospel. Our debt to a holy God is paid in full. All praise and all glory to Jesus Christ, the Lamb of God, the Redeemer of our souls.

CHRIST ON THE CROSS, DYING FOR OUR SINS, *IS* OUR SALVATION.

Final Thoughts on the Cross

When I was Mormon, people often asked me, "So, why don't you guys ever have a cross on top of your church?"

Well, I always had a two-part answer prepared for anyone who asked me this. (I'd be willing to wager that you have the same two set answers, LDS friend.) First, I'd say something like, "Well, you know, we don't want to dwell on the dead Jesus so much as the risen Lord." If that didn't satisfy my questioner, then I'd ask him or her, "If your cousin were brutally stabbed to death with a buck knife, would you put that bloody knife up on display to remember your cousin? Well, of course you wouldn't." That last one almost always did the trick and opened the door for me to explain the meaning of the spire, a symbol which to us signified our aspirations to become, through our diligent obedience and faithfulness, more like God. Why would we want to focus on a bloody cross when we could fix our minds on refining our own holiness and expediting our celestial call heavenward?

In the Bible, the cross of Jesus is represented in three distinct ways: materially, metaphorically, and metonymically. Mormons, for the most part, get the first two, but they entirely miss the third, metonymical, meaning of the cross.

Shawn McCraney, in his unique and highly useful comparative *Where Mormonism Meets Biblical Christianity Face to Face*, provides an excellent explanation of this very issue. I will give you a very brief synopsis of his explanation of the three meanings of the cross.

The *material* meaning of the cross, very simply, is that it was the object on which Jesus was put to death. Crucifixion was the primary method used for capital punishment by the Romans in that era.

Metaphorically, the cross has come to represent trials and afflictions suffered by all true disciples of Christ. Jesus said, "If any man will come after me, let him deny himself, and take up his cross daily, and follow me" (Lk 9:23).

The *metonymical* meaning of the cross, however, is the one totally lost upon most Latter-day Saints, and it is, by far, the most important. Metonymy is a figure of speech where one word is substituted for another with which it is closely associated. We may say, for example, that Moscow is not pleased with what's going on in the Middle East. What we really mean is that Russia and, more specifically, the government of Russia is not pleased. But we just say Moscow. This is metonymy.

McCraney summarizes:

> This view of the cross is perhaps the MOST important as the cross of Christ is used metonymically for the gospel, the doctrine of the gospel, and of what He did upon the cross to bring about the Good News for us. In this case, the cross is metonymical for everything the Good News represents: it's the work of Christ for man, the shed blood, the hope, the miracle, our justification, and our sanctification … it is emblematic of our very eternal life. And the Bible tells us so.
>
> —McCraney, *WMMBC*, p. 146

But apparently not everyone gets the rich, powerful, metonymical meaning of the cross. I know I didn't when I was LDS. I had a genuine disdain for people who would wear crosses around their necks at ballgames, for example, while they washed down a hot dog with a Budweiser. The nerve of those people! And don't even get me started on people with tattoos of crosses. Knowing nothing, of course, about their faith in Christ or their love and appreciation for what He did on the cross, I immediately judged them as being reckless and lousy representatives of Jesus. I was often tempted to say, "That cross tattoo does *not* make you a Christian, you know!" I never actually said that to anyone but I thought it many times.

The more common attitude of the Latter-day Saint toward the evangelical Christian, however, is to accuse him of making the gospel overly simplistic. To the Mormon, believing that it is all about the cross of Jesus is ridiculous. It just cannot be that easy. To which I always respond, "Easy for whom? Certainly not for Jesus!"

Paul encountered this very criticism virtually everywhere he went. Remember, it was Paul who wrote, "For I determined to know *nothing* among you except Jesus Christ, and Him crucified" (1 Cor 2:2, italics mine). In a sense, what he was saying was, "Look, we're not going to talk about the exodus anymore, or animal sacrifice, or sabbath worship, or any of that stuff now. It doesn't matter anymore. Let's talk about the consummation and fulfillment of all these things: Christ on the cross, paying the price for your sins."

But the Jews weren't having it, and neither were the Greeks; albeit for entirely different reasons. Paul writes, "For indeed Jews ask for signs and Greeks search for wisdom; but we preach Christ crucified, to Jews a stumbling block and to Gentiles foolishness" (1 Cor 1:22–23).

So to the Greeks, known for their deep philosophies and philosophers (Aristotle, Plato, Socrates), the cross of Jesus was just, well, dumb. It was the silliest thing they'd ever heard. It was foolishness to them, according to Paul.

But to the Jews, it was a stumbling block. That's interesting phraseology. A stumbling block is usually something solid that's lying right in front of you, in plain sight, and yet you trip and stumble right over it. The cross of Jesus was a stumbling block to the Jews because they simply could not accept that their salvation, their righteous standing with God, could possibly come down to their acknowledgment of the vicarious sacrifice of Christ on the cross. They much preferred, even as difficult as it was to observe, the Law of Moses, with its 600-plus rules and commandments!

Imagine a large family that immigrates to New York City in the 1930s from, say, the Ukraine. In addition to Mom, Dad, and the kids, the grandparents and a few of the aunts, uncles, and cousins have come along. As they get situated in their cramped, two bedroom apartment, Uncle Dmytro (the cleverest of the bunch) sets up a half dozen stationary bicycles in the smaller bedroom and hooks them up with funny looking electrical converter boxes and extensive wiring.

Every evening, once the children get home from school, the family breaks up into teams of six. And in three-hour blocks, these teams peddle their little hearts out in order to generate enough electricity to power up the lights in their apartment as well as a couple fans and an old RCA radio. This is, after all, how they had always done it in the old country.

What they fail to realize, of course, is that all they need to do is go downstairs to the front desk and request to be plugged into the city's power grid. And for the purposes of this obvious allegory, we'll say that the electricity is free for the asking.

Ridiculous? Of course. Yet this was precisely what many of the Jews in Jesus' time were doing and what many legalists still insist on doing to this day.

Conclusion

Here are some basic questions that serve as an easy diagnostic test for my reader. How do you feel about the cross? Can you say that the cross is *the* central symbol of your life? Does the thought of the cross bring joy, gratitude, security, and power into your life? Can you say that the cross of Jesus (metonymically) *is* your salvation? Is the blood of Jesus sufficient, or do you find yourself seeking to add to it?

IS THE BLOOD OF JESUS SUFFICIENT, OR DO YOU FIND YOURSELF SEEKING TO ADD TO IT?

I believe it is of critical importance that we pass this test. And I have a solid reason to base this on. Paul writes this to the saints in Corinth: "For the word of the cross is foolishness to those who are perishing, but to us who are being saved it is the power of God" (1 Cor 1:18).

So, take a minute and ask yourself these questions: Is the cross foolishness to me? Does the message of the cross seem far too simplistic for my liking? *Just believe that Jesus died for your sins and you get to go to heaven*—does this insult your intelligence or need for healthy competition? Does it bother you that a complete knucklehead who smokes cigarettes and has tattoos of naked women on his arms can also have an unshakeable faith that Christ suffered and died for his sins and gets to go to heaven too?

I know exactly how you're feeling right now, my LDS reader. It is, without a doubt, the hardest thing to come to terms with—this idea that Christ did it all. The very thought that there is nothing you can do, *nothing*, to earn any part of your salvation is almost impossible for you to grasp. Deep down, you may not even *want* to grasp it, because then where's your chance to shine? How will you ever distinguish yourself as being celestial material, for example, and not another lowly telestial guy? As Dwight Edwards writes in his phenomenal book *Revolution Within*:

> It's harder than most of us think to fully let go of a law-based approach to spirituality. Our flesh naturally gravitates toward legalistic approaches to holiness that encourage at least some reliance on self. A blend of God's helping us and our helping God is both reasonable and enticing to our fallen nature. It enables us to partially share credit with God for any spiritual success. Most of all, it keeps our pride at least somewhat intact.
>
> —Edwards, *RW*, p. 10

I hate to break it to you folks, but pride is about the last thing you want to keep intact. Take it from me. But lest my Mormon friends despair, I've got good news for you. It turns out that there *is* a role for you to play in your salvation! And it is to this role that we now turn our attention.

SECTION V
THE SOLUTION
(PART 2)

CHAPTER 10

WHOEVER BELIEVES

These things I have written to you who believe in the name of the Son of God, so that you may *know* that you have eternal life.
—1 John 5:13

One of the most dramatic scenes of the entire Bible is found in Acts 16, where we find Paul and Silas preaching the gospel and casting out demons in the city of Philippi, for which they were beaten and thrown into prison. Despite being bruised and bloodied, despite being held in tight confinement, with their feet fastened in stocks, Paul and Silas were "praying and singing hymns of praise to God" well into the night. Verse 25 tells us that the other prisoners were listening to them praise God, undoubtedly in utter astonishment.

Scripture tells us that suddenly there was a tremendous earthquake that shook the prison so powerfully that it broke open all the prison doors and even unfastened all the prisoners' chains! When the jailer awoke and saw all the doors open, he naturally assumed that the prisoners had escaped on foot. Knowing that the penalty for allowing the prisoners to break out was death, he thought he'd save himself and his family the disgrace of allowing such a breach in security and drew his sword to take his own life. Paul, seeing the desperation and panic of the jailer, called out to him, telling him not to harm himself and that he had nothing to fear. None of the prisoners had fled; they were all accounted for.

Can you imagine the relief this man must have felt? And can you imagine the gratitude and respect he must have had for Paul and Silas? It is unlikely that the jailer had ever encountered men like these two before. But there were three things about Paul and Silas he knew for certain: their trust in and love for God was unassailable; they possessed remarkable integrity, which showed in their not fleeing the prison when they could have; and they demonstrated a rare kindness and compassion for him, of all people, at the moment that he was about to take his own life.

Who were these guys? How did they come to possess such uncommon qualities? Let's pick up the action in verse 29, when the jailer approaches Paul and Silas: "And he [the jailer] called for lights and rushed in, and trembling with fear he fell down before Paul and Silas, and after he brought them out, he said, 'Sirs, *what must I do to be saved*?' They said, '*Believe in the Lord Jesus, and you will be saved*, you and your household.' And they spoke the word of the Lord to him together with all who were in his house" (Acts 16:29–32, italics mine).

"Believe in the Lord Jesus, and you will be saved …" Of all the things the jailer might have anticipated as the answer to his question about what he must do to be saved, I doubt that that was one of them. And yet we see how quickly he gravitated to this remarkably simple solution to the dilemma of his lost soul. Verse 34 says that after he washed their wounds and gave them a warm meal, the jailer "rejoiced greatly, having believed in God with his whole household."

The Bible teaches that there are essentially five things that we must do in order to enter into God's kingdom. Let's call these the five pillars of our salvation:

1. Believe
2. Repent
3. Receive
4. Abide
5. Endure

In this section, we'll discuss the first three, believe, repent, and receive. We'll pick up the other two in subsequent chapters.

"As Moses Lifted Up the Serpent"

In the previous section, we looked at John 3:16, the entire gospel encapsulated in one solitary verse: "For God so loved the world, that He gave His only begotten Son, that whoever believes in Him shall not perish, but have eternal life." But let's back up a bit and look at the conversation between Jesus and Nicodemus that led up to this amazing and radical proclamation.

Nicodemus, a highly respected "ruler of the Jews," came to Jesus by night to learn more about Him. It appears from the text that Nicodemus was primarily interested in the miracles Jesus performed and perhaps wanted to know exactly how He did them. But Jesus had no interest in talking about miracles that night. He had one thing to share with Nicodemus and one thing only: his need to be "born again" of God's Spirit. In John 3:3, Jesus answered a question that Nicodemus didn't even ask, saying, "Truly, truly, I say to you, unless one is born again he cannot see the kingdom of God."

As we read on, it's hard to say whether or not Nicodemus is genuinely stupefied by Jesus' proclamation or if he's being sarcastic. Either way, he asked Jesus how a grown man could possibly enter back into his mother's womb to be born a second time. Jesus seized the opportunity to explain to Nicodemus two important distinctions. First, this new birth is spiritual, not physical. And second, the process by which this spiritual rebirth occurs is mysterious and intangible. It cannot be quantified by material means or even described in material terms. Jesus revealed: "That which is born of the flesh is flesh, and that which is born of the Spirit is spirit. Do not be amazed that I said to you, 'You must be born again.' The wind blows where it wishes and you hear the sound of it, but do not know where it comes from and where it is going; so is everyone who is born of the Spirit" (Jn 3:6–8).

What a perfect analogy. As John MacArthur points out, "Just as the wind cannot be controlled or understood by human beings but its effects can be witnessed, so also it is with the Holy Spirit. He cannot be controlled or understood, but the proof of His works is apparent" (Notes, *MacArthur Study Bible*, 2169). We'll go into much more depth regarding what it means to be born again in Chapter 17.

Nicodemus still isn't getting it. "How can these things be?" he asks (v. 9). Jesus issues a mild rebuke, questioning the Pharisee's qualifications as a "teacher of Israel." It's obvious to Jesus that He's going to need to get a little more specific with Nicodemus, drawing upon a tangible symbol with which he would have been very familiar. Jesus goes old school on Nicodemus: "As Moses lifted up the serpent in the wilderness, even so must the Son of Man be lifted up; so that whoever believes will in Him have eternal life" (Jn 3:14–15).

What is Jesus referring to here? What's this about Moses lifting up a serpent? The answer is found in Numbers 21:6–9, where we read one of the more fascinating stories of the Old Testament, the story of the bronze serpent.

Basically, the Israelites, despite God's grace and provision, found a way to grumble and gripe against God and Moses for leading them "up out of Egypt to die in the wilderness." Angered by their ingratitude and lack of faith, God sent "fiery serpents" among them. These snakes were apparently extremely venomous because many of the Israelites were bitten by the snakes and died. Very quickly, the people repented of their wickedness and asked Moses to intervene and plead with God to remove the snakes. Moses agreed to help his people. We pick up the story in verses 8 and 9: "Then the Lord said to Moses, 'Make a fiery serpent, and set it on a standard; and it shall come about that everyone who is bitten, when he looks at it, he will live.' And Moses made a bronze serpent and set it on the standard; and it came about that if a serpent bit any man, when he looked to the bronze serpent, he lived" (Num 21:8–9).

Now, try to put yourself in the position of one of the Israelites bitten by a poisonous snake. Moses comes along and says that all you have to do is look at a bronze snake he's attached to a pole, and voila, you'll live! If you don't look at it, you'll die. *"Okay. If you say so ..."*

I imagine that many of them died unnecessarily for refusing to look at that snake! How absurd it must have seemed to them. Why on earth would just *looking* at some bronze snake save me from this venom coursing through my veins? I will confess to you that the old me, the old, prideful, arrogant me would have died a gruesome death—and I would have deserved it.

Now that we understand what Jesus was referring to, these verses make much more sense: "... even so must the Son of man be lifted up; so that *whoever believes will in Him have eternal life*" (italics mine). Of course, we have the advantage of knowing that the Son of Man was, in fact, lifted up (on a cross); Nicodemus, at that moment, did not. We also have the luxury of New Testament Scripture that repeatedly tells us that if we will look to the cross of Jesus and believe that He suffered and died for our sins, we will be saved.

On one occasion, for example, a crowd of inquiring Jews followed Jesus into Capernaum, seeking, undoubtedly, to trip Him up. Their question to Him was straightforward: "What shall we do, so that we may work the works of God?" (Jn 6:28). Jesus' response was an unambiguous pronouncement about the radical, game-changing nature of His message, His very purpose for coming into this world. "Jesus answered and said to them, 'This is the work of God, that you *believe* in Him whom He has sent'" (Jn 6:29, italics mine).

Nicodemus, like the crowd in Capernaum, had exactly one tool in his bag to achieve righteousness and make his way into heaven when he died: obedience to the Law. But at least the Law was tangible to him. He could, on an ongoing basis, measure and evaluate his performance relative to perfect obedience to the law.

Many Latter-day Saints, like the Jews of old, are more comfortable clinging to a tangible set of laws than trusting in a highly intangible and, to them, overly simplistic promise: look to the cross and believe that Jesus completed the work of your salvation there. Look to the cross and live. Look anywhere else, including to your own works and obedience, and live not. This was Jesus' message to Nicodemus that night, and it is still His message to each of us today.

LOOK TO THE CROSS AND LIVE. LOOK ANYWHERE ELSE … AND LIVE NOT.

The Biker Dude

I shared with you in a previous chapter my recollection of that very first Sunday when I walked into a non-denominational Christian church and how it struck me that those people were celebrating what God had already done for them. It seemed irreverent to me and very presumptuous. *You can't celebrate your salvation yet! It ain't over 'til it's over. Don't count your chickens before they hatch.*

This brings to mind the other image that remains with me from that first Sunday—the guy sitting next to me that day.

I told you I showed up for church wearing a shirt and tie, despite my girlfriend telling me it was overkill. And the guy sitting next to me? Well, let me try to paint an accurate picture here: burly biker dude; late 40s; shaved head but with a long, salt and pepper goatee; tattoos covering both arms (including a spider web on his left elbow—this guy had done some time); tattoos running up both sides of his neck; smoker's voice; a few missing teeth; and a smile and joyful countenance that I can still see in my mind to this very day. I never caught his name, but at the end of the service, he gave me a manly half-embrace and welcomed me to their church.

The reason I still remember him so vividly after fourteen years isn't because of his appearance or our brief interaction, per se. The fact is, I never sat by him in church or interacted with him ever again. The reason he made such an impact on me was because of what Pastor Brad taught that morning and how I originally processed that teaching.

What Pastor Brad said that day is something he incorporates into virtually every sermon he preaches on Sunday morning: that our salvation is a free gift from God. There is nothing we can do to earn it, and there is nothing we can do to lose it as long as we maintain our faith that Jesus Christ is the Son of God and that He suffered and died on a cross to pay the penalty for our sinfulness, thereby purchasing our salvation. To me at that moment, this concept was both electrifying and insulting. I loved it and hated it at the same time.

I loved it because it rang true to me. I loved it because for the first time in my life I thought that maybe I had a shot at heaven too. I had tried, for a good solid twenty years, to be good enough in God's eyes, to feel safe and secure in knowing that I was going to heaven. And yet I never really knew. The Book of Mormon taught me that we are saved by grace "after all we can do" (2 Nephi 25:23). But how could I ever really know that I had done all I could do? When do we ever know that our best is really our very best?

For me personally, trying to live out the religion of my youth was a neurotic exercise in futility. I only knew God in the third person, and not very well at that. Church had always been the middleman. I knew church, but I didn't know God. And I had never heard or given any consideration to this idea that God was willing to *give* me, as His gift to give, eternal life in His kingdom if I would just believe in Jesus and what He did for me. *Wow, could this possibly be true?*

And then suddenly, as I allowed for just the *possibility* that it could be true, I turned to the burly biker dude sitting next to me and realized the implications of Pastor Brad's sermon. *If salvation, eternal life in God's holy presence, is a free gift for anyone and everyone who puts his faith and trust in Jesus, then, by definition, I get to go to heaven. But so does* this *guy! Well, hang on just one minute here. You mean to tell me we're tied? After all those years of paying tithes, serving a two-year mission in Argentina, never missing church on Sunday (even when we were on vacation), graduating Magna Cum Laude from BYU, doing baptisms for the dead, and all the other wonderful churchy things I did for two decades—and I'm basically tied with this guy? There is just no way. From what I can tell, he's been nothing but a bad guy. I mean, he's done time in prison for crying out loud! What good stuff has he done? And now, just because he believes that Jesus died for his sins, he's granted entrance into heaven, just like that? And here he is already celebrating his entrance?*

Oh man, I don't know about this "saved by grace" stuff. This is just way, way too easy. How is a good guy like me ever going to stand out? (Funny how unwilling I was, at that particular moment anyway, to contemplate what a truly bad guy I had actually been! It was kind of like that $1,000 I had lied about in high school; I had been lying to myself all along, saying that I was a good guy.)

My spirit loved everything about Pastor Brad's message that day. My flesh (ego) hated every bit of it. My ego wanted to throw rotten tomatoes at Pastor Brad, mainly for the supreme confidence with which he was able to say, "I know that I am going to heaven when I die."

How could Pastor Brad, or any Christian for that matter, say with confidence that he *knows* he is going to heaven? I mean, isn't that just the epitome of arrogance? And wouldn't the belief that you've got it "in the bag," so to speak, breed complacency and remove any motivation to actually do good works and serve others as the Savior taught?

These are all excellent questions, and they are the most frequent questions I get from my LDS friends who want to know "what the heck" happened to me. As always, the Bible has the answers.

The Righteousness of God

Paul spends the entire first half of Romans 3 convincing his readers that no one, absolutely no one, is righteous enough to please God, let alone gain entrance into God's holy presence by being obedient to the Law. "There is none righteous, not even one," he tells us in verse 10. And his closing argument on this subject is found in verse 20: "For by the works of the law no flesh will be justified in His sight …" It sounds like we're all in the same boat—and it's taking on water!

And then, like being down to your last dime and then finding out you've just won $100 million in the lottery, everything changes in a flash. The entire letter to the Romans pivots on the very next verse: "But now *apart from the Law* the righteousness of God has been manifested, being witnessed by the Law and the Prophets, even the righteousness of God through faith in Jesus Christ for all those who believe …" (Ro 3:22–23, italics mine).

What's this … *apart* from the law? There is righteousness available to me that has nothing to do with my obedience to God's commandments? How can this possibly be? In baseball, we can calculate a player's batting average at any given moment in time. In college, we can keep track of the all-important GPA. You mean to tell me that there's a way to gauge a man's righteousness *apart* from a fixed standard, God's commandments, ordinances, and guidelines? No, the Bible doesn't exactly say that. What it does say is that there is a "righteousness of God" available to all those who believe and that, yes, it is apart from God's laws. The key word in the phrase "righteousness of God," believe it or not, is the word *of.* Stay with me.

In his letter to the Philippians, Paul fleshes out this totally counter-intuitive teaching of righteousness apart from the law. I say counter-intuitive, but in reality, to the Jews in that era, it was outright heresy! Take a moment and read Philippians 3 in its entirety. For those who don't have a Bible handy, let me give you a quick summary: Early in the chapter, Paul is saying that the deeper the true believer goes in his faith and trust in Christ, the less likely he is to put *any* confidence in his own flesh. This means simply that the believer assigns less and less value to his own ability to achieve righteousness or even please God, until finally he assigns no value to it whatsoever.

Then Paul goes on to say that, technically, if *anyone* had the right to put confidence in his own flesh, it was probably him, and he proceeds to list his bona fides: circumcised on the eighth day; from the tribe of Benjamin; a strict Pharisee; zealous in his persecution of the early Christian movement; and finally, in terms of righteousness in obeying God's law, found blameless (vv. 4–6). Wow, that's quite a resume!

But just when it looks like Paul is bragging about his amazing accomplishments and righteousness, he once again pivots. I would ask my LDS reader to pay close attention to these next three verses:

> But whatever things were gain to me, those things I have counted as loss for the sake of Christ. More than that, I count all things to be loss in view of the surpassing value of knowing Christ Jesus my Lord, for whom I have suffered the loss of all things, and count them but rubbish so that I may be found in Him, *not having a righteousness of my own derived from the Law, but that which is through faith in Christ, the righteousness which comes from God on the basis of faith ...*
>
> —Philippians 3:7–9, italics mine

I love Paul. And I am so thankful that he wrote all this down.

What is he saying here? He's saying that all of the advantages he had in his previous life as a "Hebrew of Hebrews," with his tribal heritage, circumcision, even his zeal and obedience, all of it to him was totally worthless compared to knowing Christ and being "found in Him." In my New American Standard Bible, Paul equates all of his previous deeds and privileges with "rubbish." Other versions use the word "dung."

I came to the exact same conclusion as Paul when I finally surrendered my life to Jesus Christ and was born again of God's Spirit. Missionary service? Dung. Tithing? Dung. Abstaining from tobacco and alcohol? Double dung. Nothing I had ever done could possibly compare to the joy, peace, strength, security, and love that I now experience just by knowing Jesus and being known by Him and adopted into the family of God.

Is there anything wrong with living an upright life, abstaining from drugs and alcohol, and serving as a missionary? Of course not. There is everything *right* about living this way. That's not Paul's point. His central point is found in verse 9, which I italicized above. It's worth repeating: "… not having a righteousness of my own derived from the Law, but that which is through faith in Christ, the righteousness which comes *from* God on the basis of faith" (italics mine).

The fact is, you have never been righteous, and you never will be, not when held up to the standard of God's righteousness. I know, tough love, but it's true. But Paul doesn't leave us there. He once again declares that there is a righteousness apart from our ability to obey the Law, which comes from God. We don't work to create that righteousness by doing good and resisting evil and then offering it up *to* God. He gives *us* righteousness, and the way He does this is through our faith in His Son. We call this *justification*. It is the "righteousness *from* God."

WE CALL THIS *JUSTIFICATION*. IT IS THE "RIGHTEOUSNESS *FROM* GOD."

Apparently, God always operated this way, even long before the arrival of Christ and His death on the cross. Paul makes this clear as he speaks of God's dealings with Abraham:

"For if Abraham was justified by works, he has something to boast about, but not before God. For what does the Scripture say? 'Abraham believed God, and it was credited to him as righteousness'" (Ro 4:2–3).

You see, no matter how good a man Abraham might have been, he would never have been able to boast about his goodness when compared head-to-head with the *greatness* of God. Abraham's "goodness" was not why God considered him righteous. Abraham's *faith* was credited to him as righteousness. Later, in verse 13, we read that even God's promise to Abraham was predicated on his faith: "For the promise to Abraham or to his descendants that he would be heir of the world was not through the law, but through the righteousness of faith."

Are you starting to see how this works?

Perhaps the most succinct passage in the entire New Testament on this teaching is found in Paul's letter to the saints in Ephesus: "For by grace you have been saved through faith; and that not of yourselves, it is the gift of God; not as a result of works, so that no one may boast" (Eph 2:8–9). In this one passage, Paul tells us everything we need to know about our salvation; he tells us what it is and what it is not. It is: by grace, through faith, and it is a gift from God. It is not: of ourselves (we can't make it happen) or a result of our works.

It sounds to me like God really doesn't want us to boast about, well, anything. And He does not want us to assign value, any salvation value, to our good works or obedience. Do you get that feeling too? Maybe not yet, but you will.

These verses also tell us that our faith (in Christ) *activates* God's grace unto salvation. This is echoed in Romans 5:1–2: "Therefore, having been justified by faith, we have peace with God through our Lord Jesus Christ, through whom also we have obtained our introduction by faith into this grace in which we stand …"

In other words, God is continually scanning the horizon, searching for those who find themselves sufficiently broken and lost, those who have come to that place of complete desperation, having no other option but to place their faith and trust in Jesus Christ. (It's sad, but that's usually what it takes.) And for as overly simplistic and easy as this may sound to many Latter-day Saints, the moment that a person puts his or her faith in Christ for salvation, it's done. It is finished. *Tetelestai.*

Some are offended by this. I know I was. Why should someone be able to make a complete mess of his life and do really horrible things and then just be able to say a few magic words—Oh, please save me, Jesus!—and presto, everything's okay. Well, first of all, it isn't in any "magic" words. Remember, God searches our hearts. He knows who has sincerely placed his or her faith in His Son. It is not for us to judge. And remember also that many, according to Jesus Himself, will come to Him on the day of judgment and say, "Lord, Lord. Have we not cast out demons in your name?"

But Jesus sees them for the frauds they are and dismisses them post haste: "Depart from me, workers of iniquity. I never knew you" (Mt 7:22–23). You can't *talk* your way into heaven, folks.

Metanoia

There can be no talk of saving faith, however, apart from true repentance. And when we use the word *repentance* in this context, we are referring to its meaning in the fullest sense.

When Jesus began His ministry, the very first words He uttered were recorded as being, "Repent, for the kingdom of heaven is at hand" (Mt 4:17). In the original Greek, the word here for repent is *metanoia,* which means "to change one's mind." What did Jesus mean by this? What were they to change their minds about? Because Jesus' ministry was to the house of Israel, He was asking them to change their minds about, well, nearly everything! In a sense, Jesus was preparing them for the radical changes that He was about to bring about: His fulfillment of the law, the introduction of new wine into new wineskins.

This same call of repentance, this radical change of one's mind, is as relevant to the unbeliever today as it was to the Jews (and Gentile unbelievers) in Jesus' era. For the person taking that very first step toward saving faith, it looks and sounds something like this: I am a sinner. I have lived to feed my fleshly instincts for as long as I can remember. I have looked to the pleasures and false wisdom of this world to satisfy my need for happiness and fulfillment, but, in reality, all I've done is make a mess of my life. I see now that there is nothing I can do to put my life back together again, let alone assuage the feelings of guilt I've piled up for all the awful things I've done. I have heard the message that there is a God in heaven who loves me and sent His Son, Jesus, to suffer and die in order to save me from the very mess I find myself in. I believe this message, and I'm ready to turn away from this world, away from my life of sin. I no longer want to live for myself. I want to know this God and begin to live for Him! I repent of my way of life.

This is *metanoia*. This is the repentance that leads us to salvation, and it goes hand in hand with believing. We are to believe and repent. In fact, we cannot *receive* God's gift of salvation, made possible by the blood of Jesus, unless and until we believe in this gift and repent of our former lives. This is "repentance leading to the knowledge of the truth" (2 Tim 2:24).

I like to think of this one-time act of *metanoia* as sort of "macro-repentance." It is a conscious decision, a radical, 180-degree turn from a life characterized by living for self and denying God to a life of denying self while living for God. And as anyone who has made this choice will tell you, it is a radical leap of faith!

The fact is, until someone makes this conscious choice, he or she cannot possibly make good on his or her new commitment because the only way to do so is by the power of the indwelling Spirit. But God's Spirit doesn't come in to empower and inspire until *after* one has made this conscious choice! So you see, there really *is* a tangible role we play in our own salvation—and it isn't for the faint of heart.

In Chapter 20, we will discuss in detail what I like to call "micro-repentance," to distinguish it from the macro-repentance of *metanoia* discussed above. This is the ongoing process of repentance reserved for the believer who, invariably, falls short of obeying God's commandments on a day-to-day basis. But for now, let's move on to the third pillar of our salvation.

CHAPTER 11

BUT AS MANY AS RECEIVED

> Having also believed, you were sealed in Him with the Holy Spirit of promise.
>
> —Ephesians 1:13

The third thing we must do, after turning to Christ in faith (believe) and turning away from the world (repent), is receive Him. By this, I mean receive His shed blood as payment for our sin. You might ask, aren't believing and receiving essentially the same things? Actually, no. Remember, James tells us that "the demons also believe, and shudder" (Jas 2:19). Apparently, it is possible to believe in Jesus as the Son of God and Savior of the world and not be saved. So what's the difference? They never received. We must believe *and* receive.

Don't Be a George Wilson

Dwight Edwards illustrates this perfectly in his book *Revolution Within*. He writes:

> In 1829 a man named George Wilson was arrested for robbery and murder in a heist of the U.S. mail. He was tried, convicted, and sentenced to death by hanging. Some friends intervened on his

> behalf and were finally able to obtain his pardon from President Andrew Jackson. But when Wilson was informed of his pardon, he refused it, saying he wanted to die.
>
> This left the sheriff with quite a dilemma. How could he execute a man who was officially pardoned?
>
> An appeal was made to President Jackson as to what to do? The perplexed president turned the matter over to the U.S. Supreme Court. Chief Justice John Marshall gave this ruling: "A pardon is a piece of paper, the value of which depends on its acceptance by the person implicated. Anyone under the sentence of death would hardly be expected to refuse a pardon, but if it is refused, it is no pardon."
>
> Thus George Wilson was executed on the gallows while his signed pardon lay a few hundred yards away on the sheriff's desk!

George Wilson's pardon did not exonerate him from his guilt. He was still guilty of those crimes. The pardon removed the penalty for those crimes—in his case, death by hanging. In the same way, Christ's payment for our sins by His own blood on the cross does not make us any less guilty of those sins. It removes the penalty that would ordinarily be attached to those sins—in our case, eternal punishment and separation from God. However, like George Wilson, we must apply our pardon for it to actually grant us life. It has to be received; otherwise, we die in our sins. Not a good way to go. John says it this way: "But as many as *received* Him, to them He gave the right to become children of God, even those who believe in His name" (Jn 1:12, italics mine).

Here Comes the Bride

My pastor once shared a story that helps to illustrate the kind of relationship that we can have with Christ in this life and, more importantly, the relationship we *need* to have with Him in the next.

A beautiful and energetic young woman in her mid-twenties has a serious problem: she's a "shopaholic." She just cannot resist expensive bags, shoes, and dresses. Her favorite store, as it turns out, is Robinson's-May (for those of you too young to remember this chain of stores, it was comparable to Macy's). Well, over the course of a couple years, she racks up a mountain of debt on her Robinson's-May credit card, an amount so massive that she struggles to pay even the monthly minimum!

Nasty letters and collection calls start to mount as our shopaholic sinks deeper and deeper into depression. The full weight of her predicament has finally settled upon her. A lawsuit has officially been filed.

At long last, she is summoned to a meeting with the head of the collections department at Robinson's-May corporate headquarters. As she enters the room, she comes face-to-face with five very stern and imposing figures, all dressed in expensive wool suits and silk ties. Two of them are attorneys, who are armed with stacks of invoices and unpaid credit card statements over a foot high. This is not looking good at all.

Just then, a handsome young man in his mid-thirties walks boldly into the room and sits down right next to the young woman. Wrapping his arm around her shoulders, he tenderly kisses her on the cheek. His suit and tie are more expensive than all of theirs combined, and the watch he's wearing would pay all of their salaries for a year!

"Who is this guy?" the panel wonders. For a moment, no one knows what to say.

The young woman was nervous and sweating before, but now she appears calm and confident. She turns to the panel and smiles, "I'm sorry. I'm being rude. This is my fiancé, Chad Robinson, son of Mr. Robinson and sole heir of the Robinson's-May retail empire. Now, what was this about a lawsuit?"

Isn't it ironic that when it's all said and done, it's all about *who you know*? We work hard our entire lives. We sacrifice, deny ourselves, serve others, obey God, and do everything we possibly can to "prove our worthiness" to live again with Heavenly Father, only to discover that it has absolutely nothing to do with any of those things. Don't you just hate that? Can you feel the resentment rising up within you right at this very moment? We certainly hate it when a less qualified person gets a promotion over us, all because of who he or she knows higher up in authority. We resent that. It's just not fair!

ISN'T IT IRONIC THAT WHEN IT'S ALL SAID AND DONE, IT'S ALL ABOUT *WHO YOU KNOW?*

And yet this is precisely what the Bible teaches. John wrote: "And the testimony is this, that God has given us eternal life, and this life is in His Son. He who has the Son has the life; he who does not have the Son of God does not have the life" (1 Jn 5:11–12).

Notice what John does *not* say: he who goes to church, he who pays his tithing, he who never lies, he who reads his scriptures every day, he who magnifies his calling, he who … fill in the blank with whatever you want! There's only one "he who" that has eternal life: he who has the Son. In our story, the young woman was totally defenseless before her accusers until the son (of Mr. Robinson) walked in the door. But the moment he took a seat next to her and claimed her as his, everything was okay—not because she was going to be able to redeem herself but because of who *he* was. Better said, everything was resolved that day because of who he was *in relation to* her.

A common image that runs throughout the New Testament is that of Christ as the bridegroom and His church, His "called-out ones," as His bride. This image is figurative but with real-life applications. Paul, for example, ties in this image of Christ as our groom when he dispenses very practical marriage advice to the men of Ephesus. Ephesians 5:25–26 states, "Husbands, love your wives, just as Christ also loved the church and gave Himself up for her, so that He might sanctify her, having cleansed her by the washing of water with the word ..."

As it relates to our salvation in God's kingdom, we have exactly one hope and one hope only. Like the young woman in our story, on our day of reckoning, we had better be engaged to the Son. When confronted with our mountain of sin debt, we have to be able to say, "This is my fiancé. He is the Son of God."

We look forward to all the riches of heaven, or as the Bible describes it, the "marriage supper of the Lamb." While here on this earth, however, we are merely engaged to Him. Christ came to this earth and committed His love for us when He died on the cross. This was the moment when He got down on one knee, as it were, and "popped the question." Now, having received this proposal, we have to respond. We have to say"yes"! "Yes, Lord, I want to live forever with you too." Martin Luther described this act of faith as the "yes of the heart" (Plass, *What Luther Says*, 1376).

The moment we say "yes" to Christ's wedding proposal, we are engaged to Him. He belongs to us, and we belong to Him. Furthermore, at the precise moment that we say "yes," we receive an engagement gift from the Father: justification. We are justified, made righteous, and placed in good legal standing with the Father. I am justified ... *just if I'd* never sinned! This is what it means to *receive* Christ. And this engagement, this reciprocal commitment with Christ, this "yes of the heart" replaces religion. It supersedes the law. It is, in a word, *everything* now. The true gospel of grace leads one out of religion and into relationship.

THE TRUE GOSPEL OF GRACE LEADS ONE OUT OF RELIGION AND INTO RELATIONSHIP.

"But I *have* received Jesus Christ as my Lord and Savior," my devout Mormon reader may say. And that may certainly be true for any given individual. Far from me to determine who has and who has not truly received

Christ and who has or has not been born again. Only God knows that. However, Scripture provides us with a powerful clue as to *how* one can "gain Christ," or at least one very important prerequisite for doing so.

Let's go back to Philippians 3 for a moment to identify that clue. Starting in verse 8, Paul states that he gladly "… suffered the loss of all things, and count them but rubbish *so that* I may gain Christ, and may be found in Him, not having a righteousness of my own derived from the Law, but that which is through faith in Christ, the righteousness which comes from God on the basis of faith" (Phil 3:8–9, italics mine). You see, as long as Paul was assigning value to his own efforts, his qualifications of worthiness, he was not able to gain Christ. He had to literally discard even the *thought* of having his own righteousness *so that* he could lay hold of the righteousness that "comes from God." Clearly this is an either/or proposition. We can either try to develop, through hard work, self-sacrifice, and obedience, our own righteousness, or we can receive the righteousness that comes through faith in Christ. But apparently, we cannot have both! Paul counted all of his efforts as rubbish so that he could gain the righteousness of Christ; and we must too.

The Garbage and the Gold Bricks

Imagine that you're taking the trash out one morning before work. In each hand, you're carrying a large trash bag full of garbage. Just then, your best friend comes running up to you carrying with him two shiny gold bricks. He is so excited he can barely speak. Finally, he's able to blurt out that he has won the lottery, and for starters, he wants to give you these gold bricks, each weighing twenty pounds (worth about $1 million). He's in a hurry and tells you that you've got to take them right now. But you can't right now because your hands are occupied with two large bags of garbage. What to do? Obviously you set the bags down *so that* you can grab a hold of the generous gift and go celebrate! It's a no-brainer, right? Not necessarily.

For me, after twenty years in the LDS church, one of the hardest things to come to terms with was that my best efforts were actually, in God's eyes, garbage. I knew my secret sin life was stinky garbage. But my good stuff? All my church attendance, home teaching, and monthly fasting, those are all in the trash bags too? Yes. Remember, it was Isaiah who came to this same realization that all of our best righteousness is but "filthy rags" to a holy God. And this is why I was in trouble. I thought I was holding gold (or at least gold leaf),when in reality, it was nothing but garbage. And until we empty our hands of everything that occupies them, including our belief that there is something (anything) that we can do to earn our salvation, we can never receive the gold. This is a tough one, isn't it? It took me literally nine years to come to grips with this, so be patient with yourself … but don't be *that* patient!

In fact, may I give you a shortcut that will cut about, oh, eight years and eleven months off of this process? Set the garbage bags down and stop contemplating their contents. In other words, stop thinking about yourself and your limitations. Stop thinking about your strengths too. Fix your eyes on Jesus and on Him alone. Spend time with Him. Take a month and read nothing but the Gospels. Focus all of your attention on His life, His death, and His promises. Remember, it is on the basis of faith in Christ (and His promises) that we receive righteousness (Phil 3:9). And what are those promises?

- He purchased your salvation for you on Calvary that dark day.
- The price paid for your past, present, and future sins was and is paid in full.
- His blood is sufficient … if you will but trust that.

Initially, this is difficult to do and almost terrifying. What if the Bible's wrong? What if this isn't true? What if I *do* have to be in church every Sunday, pay my tithing, and do my genealogy? For years, I did what a lot of former Mormons do; I hedged my bets. I wanted to trust that Jesus did it all, but it just seemed too easy. So I made sure I was in church every Sunday, and I attached value to my church attendance. I tithed to my church, and I attached value to that act of obedience (that was an easy one because I could literally attach a monetary value to my offering). I did nice things for people, hoping God was taking notice, and you guessed it, I attached value to those acts of kindness too. I figured God surely would approve of me more for doing those things. Right?

Actually, no. There is only one act of righteousness that has ever earned God's seal of approval, and that is "the obedience of the One," Christ on the cross, suffering and dying, spilling His precious blood to pay the penalty for the world's sinfulness. My insistence on attaching value to my hit-and-miss obedience to God's commandments, mixed in with sporadic fits of outright rebellion against God, topped off with the pride and arrogance of believing that I was somehow adding to what Christ had already done on my behalf, was just slowing down the process by which I could have received, instantaneously, the "righteousness that comes from God on the basis of faith."

The writer of Hebrews says it far better than I ever could. Hebrews 12:1–2 says, "… let us also lay aside every encumbrance and the sin which so easily entangles us, and let us run with endurance the race that is set before us, *fixing our eyes on Jesus, the author and perfecter of faith*, who for the joy set before Him endured the cross, despising the shame, and has sat down at the right hand of the throne of God" (italics mine).

There are actually even more serious ramifications to placing value on our good works and obedience. In fact, it is so important that we understand this that I've decided to dedicate the entire next section to this subject. But we'll get to that.

The *No* of the Heart

If receiving salvation as a gift from God is the "yes of the heart," what are the ways in which we say "no"? And why would anyone ever say "no"?

First, there are those who simply do not believe that God would be so generous as to offer a gift as valuable as eternal life predicated solely on our trust and faith in His Son. In other words, where else is something of such great value just given to someone based on his willingness to receive it? No one just wakes up, for example, and says, "Hey, I want a Ph.D. in nuclear physics," and *shazzam*, there you go! It just doesn't happen that way—not in the physical realm. The mistake some people make, then, is assuming that God deals with people roughly in the same way we do. But remember, God's ways are not man's ways. God's ways are higher than ours (Is 55:8,9).

Second, there are those who say "no" to God's gift because they know that with this gift comes a serious commitment. They are aware that those truly born again of God's Spirit, the true disciples of Christ, are required to "die to self," "pick up their crosses daily," and follow Him (Mt 16:24). These people accept in principle that God is offering eternal life as a free gift but, when it comes right down to it, love their sin too much to accept the offer. The flesh never wants to die to self; quite the contrary. This was me during my transition years out of religion, when I was not yet quite ready, apparently, for a relationship with Christ as Lord over my life.

And third, there are those who believe that salvation is a gift but that one has to do something to earn it or be worthy of this gift. This is Mormonism in a nutshell. Elder McConkie once wrote: "Salvation is free, but it must also be purchased; and the price is obedience to the laws and ordinances of the gospel" (*DNTC*, 3:256).

Huh? That reminds me of when I was a kid and saw a TV commercial advertising a really cool fishing pole. The spokesman said, "Call now for your *free* fishing pole; just send in $19.99 for shipping and handling."

So, to Elder McConkie, at least, salvation is free, but you still have to pay for it with your "obedience to the laws and ordinances of the gospel." This, of course, makes very little sense.

Spencer W. Kimball made no such allusion to a free salvation when he wrote, "Eternal life hangs in the balance awaiting the works of men" (*MoF*, p. 208).

In the end, either Jesus and Paul were right—salvation is a free gift for all those who believe—or McConkie and Kimball were right—salvation is a combination of God's grace *and* our obedience/good works. But can you agree with me that both sides cannot be right? Yes? Okay, then here's what you need to do now. Choose either Jesus and Paul or McConkie and Kimball. In fact, let's make this easier. Let's drop the weakest contestant on both sides, just for the sake of simplicity. Okay? So now, here are your choices: Jesus, Creator of heaven and earth, the Alpha and Omega, the Lion of Judah, Savior of the world vs. Spencer W. Kimball of Thatcher, Arizona. *Well, now that you put it that way* … Yes, I intentionally set it up this way to show you just how easy your choice can be.

The Young Couple and the Gorgeous Mansion

Charles Dickens was famous for writing alternative endings to his novels, usually two different endings but sometimes more. I'd like to use this technique to provide you with a picture illustration of how Latter-day Saints and Christians differ in their understanding of salvation (eternal life in God's presence) and the process by which salvation is gained.

First, here is the Mormon version. A young couple in their late twenties has been married for four years, and although they are very much in love, they have struggled financially from day one. Kyle works two jobs and goes to school two nights a week. Shannon also works two jobs and is trying to launch her own internet business on top of that. Even so, they struggle to make rent each month, and every time they scrape together a little money toward a down payment on a home of their own, something happens—the transmission goes out, their healthcare premiums go up, etc. Neither one is a quitter; yet each of them is quietly giving up hope of ever getting ahead.

One day, a well-dressed man with a briefcase knocks on their door. He is accompanied by a very professional-looking woman with a Century 21 badge on her coat. He introduces himself as an attorney responsible for delivering some very exciting news to the couple. He asks them if they would please join him and his realtor friend for a short ride in the limousine parked out front.

After a twenty-minute drive across town, the limousine passes through a beautiful iron gate and onto a cobblestone, circular driveway. Kyle and Shannon step out of the limo and look up to see the most spectacular

Tuscan-style mansion they have ever seen. It is beautifully landscaped and has custom stonework. It is a dream house by any standard! They ask, "What is this all about?"

The attorney invites them up to the front porch, hands them an envelope, an expensive pen, and a set of keys. Trying to conceal his own excitement, he says, "Kyle, your Uncle Fred, as I'm sure you know, is a very wealthy man. He loves you both very much and just could not bear to watch you kids struggle any more. He sent me here to deliver these keys over to you and to tell you 'Congratulations! The house is yours.'"

Stunned by this news, Kyle and Shannon are speechless. They just cannot believe that Uncle Fred would do this for them. Kyle had always loved his uncle, but it had been years since he had seen him, owing mainly to the fact that Fred lived on the East Coast; whereas they had always lived in California. And yet here they were, about ready to take a tour of their new multi-million-dollar estate!

Before they enter the house, however, the attorney asks if they would just take a moment to sign some documents, loan documents to be exact.

Loan documents? Hmmm, what's this all about? The celebration comes to a screeching halt as the kids start thumbing through the paperwork and, in particular, the mortgage coupon book. Suddenly it becomes clear that what Uncle Fred did was make the *down payment* on the house; he hadn't purchased it outright. And although this down payment was incredibly generous in its own right, it left Kyle and Shannon with a crushing monthly obligation. In fact, it was several times more than what they were paying in rent! How would they ever manage?

Not wanting to seem ungrateful, yet needing some time alone to talk all this over, the kids excuse themselves from the attorney and realtor. After a lengthy discussion, they decide they'll just have to redouble their efforts to somehow make this work. Kyle will quit school and take a third job. Shannon will seek investors to jump start her fledgling business. But one way or the other, they commit to making the monthly mortgage if it kills them.

And this, for all practical purposes, is the Mormon version of salvation. It says that Christ's sacrifice in the garden and on the cross makes it possible for everyone to be saved in God's kingdom. He made the down payment with His own blood on our behalf. Our job, then,is to faithfully make the mortgage payment every month for the rest of our lives. We do this by being obedient to all of God's commandments and participating in all of His ordinances while here on this earth. And there is very little room for error or omission. When we do err, there is repentance. With regards to ordinances (baptism, endowment, etc.), these are non-negotiable; we must perform them.

Elder Bruce R. McConkie once wrote, "Salvation comes by obedience to the whole law of the whole gospel. Thus, a man may be damned for a single sin!" (*DNTC*, 3:256). This is kind of like missing a mortgage payment or two; that's when you find out who really owns the house. This is why the Latter-day Saint rarely, if ever, will celebrate his or her salvation: the home isn't paid off yet. Celebrating one's salvation while the trials and temptations of life are still ongoing, to the Latter-day Saint, would be like a football player celebrating a touchdown before he gets into the end zone. He just might, in the process of celebrating, lose his grip on the ball and fumble it away! It's also why LDS church meetings never feel like a celebration. Rather, they serve as a time for instruction—how to best utilize one's resources, both spiritual and temporal, in order to make that monthly payment.

THIS IS WHY THE LATTER-DAY SAINT RARELY, IF EVER, WILL CELEBRATE HIS OR HER SALVATION.

Now, let's look at the biblical Christian version of the story. For the sake of time, let's pick up our story at the front porch, but this time, the attorney extends to the couple an envelope and a set of keys only. No pen.

The attorney nervously clears his throat, trying to conceal his excitement but not doing a very good job of it. "Kyle," he begins, "Your Uncle Fred loves you both very much. He just could not watch you struggle another day, and so he has purchased this home for you. It gives me great pleasure to hand over to you the trust deed and the keys to your new home. Congratulations!"

Stunned silence. Neither Kyle nor Shannon can believe what has just happened.

"When you say that Uncle Fred has purchased this home for us, what exactly does that mean?" Kyle asks.

"Uh, well, it means just that, Kyle. He bought this house for you, and now it's yours. Free and clear. Paid in full. The trust deed you're holding makes it official," the attorney responds.

Still incredulous, Kyle persists, "But what's our role in this? Certainly there's something we have to do to have a home like this."

The attorney holds out the keys once again and says, "There *is* one thing you have to do; take these keys. Take these keys, open this door here, and enjoy your new life. That's it."

Now the celebration kicks into full gear! And although life isn't without trials and difficulties for Kyle and Shannon, it is just a whole lot better in their beautiful mansion. They are safe and secure, lacking for nothing.

Now, for a minute, let's imagine that dear Uncle Fred, in order to be closer to his favorite nephew and his wife, moves out to California and buys a home just a few minutes away from them. He wants nothing more than to enjoy a close relationship with them as his life draws to a close. How do you think Kyle and Shannon would feel toward Uncle Fred? Can you even imagine the love and gratitude they'd have for him? Is there anything they wouldn't do for Uncle Fred? Of course not!

And so it is with the forgiven sinner, the person born again of God's Spirit. That person's acts of worship, his obedience, his service in God's kingdom are merely by-products of his salvation. The true Christian strives to live a life that brings honor and glory to God, and the fuel for that desire is a profound gratitude for what God has already given: eternal life in His kingdom!

Christianity is the only religion (although I hate to use that word) that starts at the finish line. Salvation is guaranteed up front! And every bit of obedience and good work flows *from* that salvation as opposed to the LDS teaching, which is that obedience and good works are necessary *for* salvation. We'll delve much deeper into this critical distinction later in the book.

CHRISTIANITY IS THE ONLY RELIGION … THAT STARTS AT THE FINISH LINE. SALVATION IS GUARANTEED UP FRONT!

Finally, let's imagine Uncle Fred moving out to California in the Mormon version of the story. Kyle and Shannon are still very grateful to him for generously making the down payment, and yet, for as much as they'd love to spend quality time with him, they're both extremely busy working three jobs! And when Uncle Fred does come over to visit, they feel a certain degree of pressure to appear happy and delighted with the home. But the fact is, their fear of losing the home by not being able make the mortgage payment produces a strain in their relationship with Uncle Fred, which is the last thing either of them wants. They just hope it doesn't show.

Does every Latter-day Saint feel this way toward God and about his or her salvation? Probably not, but I know I sure did. Consider the following explanation of salvation on the official church website, www.LDS.org (italics added):

> Those who have been baptized and received the gift of the Holy Ghost through the proper priesthood authority have been conditionally saved from sin. In this sense, *salvation is conditional,*

> *depending on an individual's continuing in faithfulness*, or enduring to the end in keeping the commandments of God. Individuals cannot be saved in their sins; *they cannot receive unconditional salvation simply by declaring a belief in Christ with the understanding that they will inevitably commit sins throughout the rest of their lives.*

Oh, okay. No pressure then. Just be sure not to commit sins throughout the rest of my life—or even admit that it's inevitable. You want me to pay a $10,000 a month mortgage? Piece of cake.

CHAPTER 12

THE DIVINE EXCHANGE

"Behold, I am making all things new."

—Revelation 21:5

So here we are. We talked about *the dilemma*, which is that we desire to be in God's holy presence and yet are unable to do so because of our self-disqualifying sinful nature. We talked about how Christ came to absorb the penalty for our sinfulness so that we could, in fact, be made righteous and pure, able to not only withstand the consuming fire of God's holiness but also to live comfortably in His presence. And finally, we talked about how we receive this righteousness by faith the moment we come to place our full trust in the redeeming blood of Christ. In other words, we come to recognize that eternal life is a gift that, unlike other gifts, cannot be purchased. It was already purchased on our behalf by God (the Son) on the cross of Calvary.

This, then, leads us to the most unimaginably powerful, life-changing truth ever revealed to man. We call it the *divine exchange*. Paul, in his second letter to the Corinthians, sums it up perfectly in one sentence: "He [God] made Him [Jesus] who knew no sin to be sin on our behalf, so that we might become the righteousness of God in Him" (2 Cor 5:21). Read this verse as many times as you need to in order to let it sink deep into your heart. Read it fifty times if that's what it takes. Christ *became* sin as He suffered and died on the cross so that the full measure of God's wrath toward sin could be fully absorbed. And then, as if that weren't enough, He turned right around and imparted His righteousness to anyone and everyone willing to accept His payment for their sin. This is remarkable.

You might think this is just too good to be true. *I give Him garbage, and He gives me gold?* Yes. *Well that's just amazing!* Yes it is. It is amazing grace. Dwight Edwards puts it this way: "If grace makes sense to you, I doubt you're close enough to really see it. The real thing defies comprehension … but not experience. Grace is God's irrational, unimaginable kindness. Grace is the most unreasonable thing in the world. It is also the most powerful and nothing is more effective for transforming lives" (*RW*, p. 73).

God loves paradoxes. I don't know why that is, but even the casual student of the Bible will see that His grand plan of redemption is replete with ironies and paradoxes. The meek shall inherit the earth (Mt 5:5). The first shall be last, and the last shall be first (Mt 20:16). The foolish things of this world shall confound the wise (1 Cor 1:27). And on the grandest of scales, the righteous Christ becomes sin so that sinful man can become righteous.

The great Bible teacher John MacArthur wrote, "As Christ was not a sinner, but was treated as if he were, so believers who have not yet been made righteous (until glorification) are treated as if they were righteous" (NASB, p. 2421).

I have discovered over the years that my LDS friends have little trouble with the first part of the divine exchange, Jesus taking upon Himself the sins of the world. It is the second part of the exchange that they often cannot accept, the *imputed* righteousness of Christ. This, of course, when viewed in the context of Mormon theology and everyday living, is not only too good to be true, but also it is entirely disruptive to the process of proving one's worthiness to return to live with Heavenly Father. Actually, it goes far beyond being disruptive; the imputed (gifted) righteousness of Christ makes the entire process unnecessary!

This was, as we talked about earlier, a stumbling block to the Jews. What were they to do with the Law of Moses if righteousness was now a gift through the cross of Jesus? Remember, Paul wrote that Jesus "took away the Law … nailing it to the cross." The Jews, then, in order to sustain their religious system, had only one option: reject the cross (to which the Law was supposedly nailed).

Technically, the Jews had no excuse for this rejection. Their very own prophets had foretold of the life and death of Messiah in exquisite detail. They also told of the imputed righteousness that would be made available by Messiah's life and death.

David foresaw the glory of heaven and the way in which true believers would be able to one day enjoy that glory. He wrote, "How blessed are the people who know the joyful sound! O Lord, they walk in the light of Your countenance. In Your name they rejoice all the day, and *by Your righteousness they are exalted*" (Ps 89:15–16, italics mine).

I am exalted by Christ's righteousness and not my own? Yes, indeed. This is the imputed righteousness of Christ. *No one is asking me to produce righteousness from within myself?* Correct again. In fact, you're not even capable of doing so. Remember, not only are you incapable of swimming to Japan from California, but also you're drowning in a sea of your own *un*righteousness.

I AM EXALTED BY CHRIST'S RIGHTEOUSNESS AND NOT MY OWN?

Isaiah uses a beautiful metaphor to make this point: "For He has clothed me with garments of salvation, He has wrapped me with a robe of righteousness" (Is 61:10). Those who come to saving faith in Jesus Christ are, in that very moment, wrapped securely in the robe of *His* righteousness. And it is the most beautiful, elegant robe ever tailored. The fabric is exquisite in its quality and the colors resplendent. Dwight Edwards describes the effect upon those who wear the robe: "We are now clothed in the robes of God's righteousness! This brings a humble, grateful dignity. The dignity comes from knowing we can approach the throne of grace with confidence. The humility comes from knowing we had absolutely nothing to do with this worthiness" (*RW*, p. 63).

I will tread very lightly here, but I believe it is worth noting the stark contrast between the "garments of salvation" mentioned in Isaiah and the garments of the Holy Priesthood introduced by Joseph Smith in Nauvoo, Illinois.

The garments worn by devout Latter-day Saints are, for the most part, symbolic in their function. They serve as a constant reminder to the people wearing them of their covenants made with God in the temple. We could debate the merits of this form of daily worship/sacrifice, but that's not really what I want to emphasize here. My point is that the LDS garments suggest to the conscious and subconscious mind that, hey, I can do this! I can obey God's commandments. I can resist alcohol, foul language, and sex outside the bonds of marriage. And when I am weak, I have these undergarments to remind me that I am better than this. I am elect, and I'm proving it through my keeping of the stringent covenants made in the temple. I am righteous … or at least, I'm getting there.

Am I far off here, Mormon friends? I don't think so. You can research for yourself in the official church handbook what the stated purpose of the garments is, and you will find that, essentially, it is to protect you physically and spiritually, safeguarding your personal righteousness.

In the final analysis, the Latter-day Saint believes that he can clothe himself with a symbol of his own righteousness. The Christian would say, "No, thanks. My *best* righteousness is but filthy rags. I prefer to be wrapped in the robe of Christ's righteousness. It suits me much better!"

Conclusion

Now, if you think the divine exchange was challenging, wait until you see what's coming next. As it turns out, attempting to prove your worthiness to return to live with God someday is not only unnecessary, but also it is altogether counter-productive. In fact, it is deadly, and the Bible tells us so. This is beyond counter-intuitive to the Latter-day Saint; it is a punch right in the gut. But it so critical that we understand this that I've decided to spend the entire next section on this one issue. So get your Bible out, please, and we'll look together at this one issue and the one book that changes *everything*.

SECTION VI
GRACE PLUS WORKS

CHAPTER 13

THE GIFT OF GOD

... do not be subject again to a yoke of slavery.

—Galatians 5:1

In his long and trial-filled ministry, Paul was accused of many things. Some saw him as foolish and even a traitor for focusing his attention on the pagan Gentiles. Some accused him of "going along to get along" when he agreed to shave his head and receive ceremonial washing in order to enter the temple in Jerusalem. Festus, the Roman governor over Judea, literally thought that Paul had gone insane! But the one thing they could never accuse Paul of was being a legalist. If anything, his consistent, against-the-grain teaching on the principle of grace made him a living, breathing lightning rod of controversy. Yet he never gave in, not one inch, to those who insisted that man must do his part to merit salvation.

In the last section we touched briefly on the core passage in Paul's letter to the Ephesians that most succinctly describes our salvation: "For by grace you have been saved through faith; and that not of yourselves, it is the gift of God; not as a result of works, so that no one may boast. For we are His workmanship, created in Christ Jesus for good works, which God prepared beforehand so that we would walk in them" (Eph 2:8–10). In this one powerful passage, we discover *what* our salvation is—the gift of God, *how* we are saved—by the grace of God, and *why* we are saved—for the glory of God (we are, after all, His "workmanship"). Let's take a moment to discuss the *what* and the *why* of our salvation, and then we'll spend the balance of this section on the *how* (and the *how not*).

Paul says unequivocally that our salvation "is the gift of God" and that this gift is predicated on His grace. Let's not make this complicated. A gift is a gift. It is unearned and, in many cases, unmerited. In fact, one of the best definitions of *grace* is "God's unmerited favor." *Mercy* is not receiving the punishment we deserve. *Grace* is receiving rewards we most certainly do not deserve! Grace goes miles beyond mercy.

GRACE IS RECEIVING REWARDS WE MOST CERTAINLY DO NOT DESERVE! GRACE GOES MILES BEYOND MERCY.

Imagine that it's your best friend's birthday, and this year is a milestone in that he's turning fifty. You've saved up some cash and gone the extra mile in buying him a nice watch and premium tickets to an upcoming ballgame—it's the playoffs! He opens your generous gift and is just floored.

"Wow! I cannot believe you got me tickets to this game! And the watch … it is just beautiful. Man, this must have set you back a pretty penny," he says.

"Well, hey," you respond, "what are best friends for? Happy birthday, man."

"No, seriously, what are we talking about here? A grand? $1,500?" Now he's digging into his pocket for his wallet. "Let me pay you something," he insists.

Now it's getting a little uncomfortable.

"Dude, what are you doing? It's your birthday. This is my gift to you. You know, b-i-r-t-h-d-a-y g-i-f-t. Put your wallet away!" you counter.

"Oh no, no, no. Let me give you half at least." He is really digging his heels in at this point. He pulls $700 out of his wallet and shoves it into your coat pocket. "Here's half," he proudly announces.

At this moment, you realize that he's dead serious; he is not going to receive your gift but rather is insisting on paying for it. In fact, the gift is no longer a gift at all. Furthermore, he's removed all the joy in both the giving and receiving of this "gift."

Obviously, this scenario is ridiculous. I tell this hypothetical story simply to underscore the absurdity of trying to pay for something that is intended as a gift. However, this little exchange also serves to help us understand why it is that our attempts at trying to earn our salvation, when it clearly is a gift from our loving Father, are displeasing to Him. Our attempts negate the gift. And when we negate God's gift, we negate God's grace, at least as it operates in our lives. Not a really good way to go. This is what Paul is driving at in Romans 11:6, when he writes, "But if it is by grace, it is no longer on the basis of works, otherwise grace is no longer grace."

Clearly this is an either/or proposition. Salvation is either achieved on the basis of works (and obedience), as it most certainly was under the Mosaic Law, or it is received on the basis of God's grace. But it cannot be both. These are mutually exclusive concepts. Otherwise, grace is "no longer grace." What God is saying essentially is this: My gift is through His blood. Period. Now, can you please accept this gift by faith so that we can get on with the business of enjoying rich fellowship with each other in My kingdom?

MY GIFT IS THROUGH HIS BLOOD. PERIOD.

Many of the early converts to Christianity, of course, were Jews. So we can certainly understand why this was such a difficult concept for them to grasp; they had lived and struggled under the law for 1,500 years! It was all they knew. But what I find fascinating and unfortunate is that now, 2,000 years after Christ fulfilled the law, "nailing it to the cross," some people (and some religions) still insist on reinserting aspects of the Law into God's *free gift* of eternal life. According to Paul, this is ill-advised. (We'll cover much more on this shortly.)

Now let's look at what the Bible teaches us regarding *why* we are saved. I will give fair warning to my LDS reader: this is a difficult one. It's difficult because of the way in which LDS teachings condition one's mind. By that I mean this: everything about the LDS *Plan of Salvation* is centered on the individual. *You* are the literal spiritual offspring of Heavenly Father and a Heavenly Mother in the pre-mortal existence. *You* chose to come to this earth to receive a body and to be tested. According to God's plan, *you* may, through strict obedience to the laws and ordinances of the gospel, be found worthy to return to His presence in the celestial kingdom. And in due time, through the principle of eternal progression, *you* will become as God, ruling and reigning over your own creation, populating your own world with your own spirit children. Does that sound about right to you?

The Bible teaches the exact opposite: it's not *at all* about you. It's all about God and His glory. Now, don't get me wrong; we matter very much to God. He created us. He pursues us. He provides for us. He even sent His Son to die for us. In short, we are very, very high on God's short list of priorities. But we are not number one. Let's say we're a close second. As Dwight Edwards points out: "You see, an infinitely perfect God must supremely value that which is of supreme value. If He doesn't, He's no longer perfect. If God were to value people over His name, the inversion would disqualify Him from being God" (*RW*, p. 30).

Nowhere in Scripture is this more powerfully depicted than in Ezekiel 36. Basically, God's chosen people, the children of Israel, had profaned the holy name of God by falling into idolatry, intermarrying with the pagans of surrounding nations, and essentially doing nothing to distinguish themselves from the sinful ways of the non-believers. It caused those non-believers to look upon Israel and ask, "*These* are the people of the Lord …?" (v. 20, italics mine). This was entirely unacceptable to the God of Israel, and so He decided to clean house.

The insights we gain into His mind in this passage are unambiguous. Let's pick up God's narrative in verse 22:

> Therefore say to the house of Israel, Thus says the Lord God, It is not for your sake, O house of Israel, that I am about to act, but for My holy name, which you have profaned among the nations where you went. I will vindicate the holiness of My great name which has been profaned among the nations, which you have profaned in their midst. Then the nations will know that I am the Lord, declares the Lord God, when I prove Myself holy among you in their sight.
>
> —Ezekiel 36:22–24

Notice how God declares that He will prove *Himself* holy. At no point are the children of Israel declared holy; but they are redeemed. In fact, when we continue on from verses 25–27, we see the work of redemption that God performs—all to His glory: "Then I will sprinkle clean water on you, and you will be clean; I will cleanse you from all your filthiness and from all your idols. Moreover, I will give you a new heart and put a new spirit within you; and I will remove the heart of stone from your flesh and give you a heart of flesh. I will put My Spirit within you and cause you to walk in My statutes …"

So, essentially, the Israelites messed everything up. Yet who came in and set things right? Who proved His worthiness? God did. God did it all, and He did it to preserve and uphold His holy name.

Six hundred years later, God would come in the flesh and do it all again, once and for all, on the cross at Calvary. And once again, He and He alone deserves all the praise and glory. Paul is so adamant about making sure we understand who gets the praise for the redemption of mankind that he mentions it four times in the first thirty verses of his letter to the Ephesians. In Ephesians 1:5–6, for example, we learn that we are adopted as children of God, through Christ, "according to the kind intention of His will, to the praise of the glory of His grace." It is to the praise of *His* glory, not ours. Remember, God designed it this way so that we would not boast in ourselves and our own works of righteousness. It is far healthier to view our own works as garbage *so that* we may gain Christ and His righteousness. Is this starting to come together now?

Let me conclude this segment with the New Testament equivalent of the Ezekiel 36 house cleaning performed by God. Take note of who the bad guys are and who does all the work to save the day as we read Ephesians 2:3–7:

> Among them we too all formerly lived in the lusts of our flesh, indulging the desires of the flesh and of the mind, and were by nature children of wrath, even as the rest. But God, being rich in mercy, because of His great love with which He loved us, even when we were dead in our transgressions, made us alive together with Christ (by grace you have been saved), and raised us up with Him and seated us with Him in the heavenly places in Christ Jesus, so that in the ages to come He might show the surpassing riches of His grace in kindness toward us in Christ Jesus.

GOD GETS ALL THE PRAISE AND GLORY BECAUSE HE DOES ALL THE WORK.

So, to summarize, God gets all the praise and glory because He does all the work. It's as simple as that. And He deserves all the glory because He and He alone is worthy of it. Dwight Edwards puts it this way:

> When God is approached primarily as the great Fixer of life, with *our* needs as His prime agenda, our lives will not only fail to reflect His glory, but we'll also fail to experience change and fulfillment in the deepest, richest sense. However, when we delight most in the spectacularness of God, when His glory becomes our highest agenda, we find a taste that thrills our souls plus we experience a nonstop transformation in our lives along the way.
>
> —*RW*, p. 31

I am experiencing this very transformation in my own life, and it began the moment I saw the absurdity of trusting in myself and the futility of trying to prove my own worthiness to a holy God. Finally, I understand why Jesus said, "But seek first His kingdom and *His righteousness*, and all these things will be added to you" (Mt 6:33, italics mine). Jesus would never be so foolish as to encourage us to seek our own righteousness; it's simply not there.

CHAPTER 14

GRACE—GOD'S UNIMAGINABLE KINDNESS

> O taste and see that the Lord is good …
>
> —Psalm 34:8

So we've talked about what our salvation is (a gift from God) and why we are saved (for the glory and praise of God). We need to spend a little time discussing *how* we are saved. We are told that it is by the grace of God. But what exactly is grace, and why is it so hard for some of us to receive it? Why would anyone be resistant to it?

A couple of years ago, my parents hosted a reunion and invited several families that we were really close to during my high school years. My dear friend and bishop during that time was there with his wife and their eldest daughter. Bishop C was sharing with me some of the highlights of a talk he had given recently on forgiveness. Specifically, he was sharing his thoughts about Jesus' encounter with the woman caught in the act of adultery. It fascinated me that, despite correctly quoting Jesus as saying, "Neither do I condemn thee," his comment to me was, "Well, of course we know that Jesus didn't *actually* forgive her …"

I wish I could remember everything Bishop C said after that, but sadly, I cannot. I listened respectfully, offered my understanding of forgiveness and grace, and then we moved on to something else. But that one conversation, more than anything else, reminded me of the Mormon mindset regarding sin, repentance, and God's grace. It also served as additional motivation to write this book.

Latter-day Saints struggle even more with Jesus' interaction with the thief on the cross than with His interaction with the adulterous woman. In fact, I submit that this one brief conversation between the dying criminal and the Savior of this world, as recorded in Luke 23:42–43, best illustrates the dramatic difference between the LDS view and the Christian view of salvation.

Here's the story: After rebuking the first criminal for mocking Jesus, this thief turns his attention to the innocent man in the middle and pleads, "Jesus, remember me when You come in Your kingdom!"

And Jesus said to him, "Truly I say to you, today you shall be with Me in Paradise."

To the Christian, this is one of the most beautiful exchanges ever recorded. This man, having made a mess of his life through a career of crime, recognizes his own sinful nature and his current predicament before a holy God. And somehow (and we're not told how), he has come to recognize Jesus for who He is: King. Fortunately,the man has the humility of heart and the good sense to reach out to Jesus, even at this late hour, and beg the King for mercy. What he got, of course, was grace. Jesus Christ, Creator of the heavens and earth, the Alpha and Omega, God in human form (and never more human than in this moment, bloody and broken on the cross) looks directly into the heart of this man, sees precisely what He's looking for—a truly penitent heart, and forgives him all his sins in that very moment. And then, putting into place the very divine exchange we discussed earlier, Jesus grants the man eternal life as His gift to give. How electrifying is that? My heart leaps for joy when I contemplate the amazing grace extended to the thief on the cross. It's beautiful.

How does the Latter-day Saint interpret this exchange? First of all, Jesus isn't actually forgiving the man. Jesus couldn't possibly forgive him because the thief cannot go through the proper steps of repentance in order to merit His forgiveness. He may, for example, have true godly sorrow, but he cannot make restitution for the sins he's committed because he's never getting down off that cross! So, essentially, he and Jesus are at a stalemate. But don't worry;Jesus, according to LDS teaching, by telling the thief that later that very day he will be with Him in paradise, is letting the thief know that he'll have an opportunity to hear the *fullness* of the gospel in paradise (better known as spirit prison). Apparently, accepting Christ's sacrifice (which for this man was happening literally right before his eyes) and placing his complete trust in Jesus as the only way into heaven wasn't enough, according to Joseph Smith. This man's going to have the opportunity to hear the *good stuff* later, in paradise.

Years ago, I took a New Testament course at BYU as part of my religion requirement. It wasn't a particularly good course, and I don't remember much about my professor—except for one particular lecture. He was trying to explain the difference between a life well lived and one marked with sin. Using a 400-meter race around an oval track as a metaphor, the professor insisted that the winner of the race would be the one who ran swiftly and didn't fall down. The guy that stumbled and fell (the sinner, for our purposes) could finish the race, but he would never catch up to the leader. He could never win the race.

To the Latter-day Saint, this makes perfect sense because the race is all about *me*. I have to win this race, and my foot speed, combined with my ability to not fall down (avoid sin), will qualify me for exaltation in the highest level of the celestial kingdom. And although I am not competing against anyone else, per se, I am competing against God's standards of righteousness and hoping to land myself a gold medal. I'll leave the silver (terrestrial) to those who just can't run as fast as I can and the bronze (telestial) to those who stumble and fall.

This explains why "death-bed repentance" is so repugnant to most Mormons. Why should I work hard my entire life, sacrifice of myself and my resources through missionary work and tithing, deny myself through strict obedience to God's commandments, and perform acts of service to others every day, just to see some knucklehead come to his senses at the last moment and repent of his sins? You mean to tell me that when it's all said and done, the knucklehead and I are on equal footing before God?

No, I am not telling you that. Jesus is.

The Parable of the Laborers

Take a minute to read Matthew 20:1–16, Jesus' famous Parable of the Laborers. For those of you who might not have a Bible handy, let me give you a brief summary of this powerful allegory. But first, let me give you a little background that will help put this parable into context.

A rich young ruler had approached Jesus and His disciples one day and asked what he needed to do to obtain eternal life. Jesus told him to keep God's commandments: don't murder or steal or commit adultery or lie. Also, honor your parents and love your neighbor. The young man responded by saying that, essentially, he was doing pretty well in all those areas and asked if there was anything else he lacked. Jesus' answer was a haymaker: go and sell all that you have, give all the proceeds to the poor, and come follow me!

Verse 22 says, "But when the young man heard this statement, he went away grieving; for he was one who owned much property." I find it fascinating that his reaction was not one of anger or rebellion or pride. He went away sad. My sense is that he *knew* Jesus was divine and, at the very least, worth following. But he just loved his material possessions too much, and so he went away grieving—grieving the missed opportunity of a lifetime.

But even more telling is the reaction of the disciples. *Goodness gracious*, they must have been thinking, *who can ever get into heaven then?* Here was a pretty righteous man, innocent of all the major areas of sin under the law, at least, and yet that wasn't enough? Jesus required him to sell all that he had? Verses 25 and 26 read, "When the disciples heard this, they were very astonished and said, 'Then who can be saved?' And looking at them Jesus said to them, 'With people this is impossible, but with God all things are possible.'"

"With people this is impossible." What does Jesus mean by that? I think He means that with people this is impossible. He does not just say it's hard, tricky, or extremely taxing. The word is *impossible*. It would be difficult to communicate more clearly than this. In this particular case, it was a wealthy young man who loved his money more than God. For someone else, it's drugs and alcohol. And for another, it's the pride of intellectualism. Whatever the stumbling block may be, we (mankind) simply are not able to overcome it. Our goal to obey God's laws, doing all the right things and avoiding all the bad things, is not and never has been realistic. Remember, Romans 8:3 says, "For what the Law could not do, weak as it was through the flesh, God did; sending His own Son in the likeness of sinful flesh as an offering for sin ..."

In other words, the law has always been unsuccessful in persuading us to obey God. But it's not the law's fault; it's our fault, our flesh's fault. Our sin nature is like gravity; it constantly pulls us down toward our base desires. Only God, through the redeeming power of Christ, can overcome that downward pull. Hence, with God, "all things are possible."

Now, we can acknowledge through our own observations the tremendous range of human good and evil. Some people are not very rebellious by nature and tend to submit to God's will for their lives quite easily. These people are rare, but we do encounter them from time to time. Other folks just seem to rush into all sorts of trouble continually—drugs, promiscuity, deceit, etc. And finally, we have the hardened criminals—rapists, murderers, and the like. Sometimes it's hard to believe we're all part of the human race, when one considers the vast sliding scale of morality represented by the Adolph Hitlers and Mother Theresas of the world. And yet here we all are … one big, hopeless family.

Jesus, of course, was also well aware of the sliding scale and, more importantly, of our tendency to compare ourselves to one another on that scale. One might say, "I go to church every Sunday, fast once a month, and help out down at the old folk's home from time to time. And I don't swear, drink alcohol, or go to strip clubs. Surely I have put myself in good standing with God. At least I'm better than *that guy*. He rarely goes to church, never tithes, and has a mouth like a truck driver. I am far more worthy than *that guy*." But Jesus, in one master stroke, demolishes this mindset and establishes the truth of God's grace with the powerful parable of the laborers.

He begins, "For the kingdom of heaven is like a landowner who went out early in the morning to hire laborers for his vineyard. When he had agreed with the laborers for a denarius for the day, he sent them into his vineyard" (Mt 20:1–2).

Those familiar with this story will recall that, after about three hours, the landowner realizes he still lacks the manpower to get the job done that day with the workforce he's hired. And so he goes back to the marketplace, finds a few other guys standing around, and hires them to come work in his vineyard too. It is important to note that the landowner does not specify the wage he's willing to pay this later group. We read in verse 4, "You also go into the vineyard, and whatever is right I will give you. And so they went." In telling the story, Jesus intentionally keeps the wages vague for all but the first group.

Well, three hours later, the landowner still lacks men to work in his vineyard, and so he repeats this same process. And he does so again three hours after that. Finally, in one last push to harvest all those grapes before the sun goes down, the landowner goes back to the marketplace and hires one last group of men with literally one hour left in the workday. So, to summarize, we have probably a few dozen men who worked in this man's vineyard that day; some worked for twelve hours, some for nine, some for six, some for three, and some worked just that one last hour of the day.

As the sun went down, the landowner calls over his foreman and asks him to pay all the workers their wages, beginning with the last group that worked just the one hour. And here's where it gets interesting, because the foreman hands each of the eleventh hour hired guns a denarius each. Well, as you can imagine, the fellas that worked the full twelve hours are thinking, "Hot diggity dog! If these last guys got paid a denarius for just one hour's work, there's no telling how much we're going to get." But, as we see in verse

10, each and every one of the workers that day received exactly the same wage—one denarius—even the guys that worked twelve hours.

Let's pick up the conversation between the disgruntled twelve-hour laborers and the landowner, starting in Matthew 20:11:

> When they received it, they grumbled at the landowner, saying, "These last men have worked only one hour, and you have made them equal to us who have borne the burden and the scorching heat of the day." But he answered them, "Friend, I am doing you no wrong; did you not agree with me for a denarius? Take what is yours and go, but I wish to give to this last man the same as to you. Is it not lawful for me to do what I wish with what is my own? Or is your eye envious because I am generous?" So the last shall be first, and first last.

In this one powerful story, Jesus covers so much of the gospel of grace that it's hard to know where to begin. Clearly, the landowner represents God, and the laborers represent us (people). The disgruntled twelve-hour laborers exemplify a certain subset of people, who we'll call *religionists*. They believe their hard work in the field (obedience, good works, and self-sacrifice) has earned them the right to greater compensation from God. But greater than whom? Greater than those who haven't worked nearly as hard or been as righteous. Let's face it, if the story here were just one of a landowner contracting with some workers for a denarius for the day and the subsequent payout of that one denarius, where would the lesson be? There'd be no controversy. If later workers had never been hired, would the original workers have ever grumbled at all? Of course not. They received exactly what they had agreed to. So, this parable isn't really about a perceived injustice. This is about resentment toward God's grace. As always, Jesus was and is testing hearts.

AS ALWAYS, JESUS WAS AND IS TESTING HEARTS.

How *do* you feel about the woman caught in the act of adultery and Jesus' unexpected grace and forgiveness poured out onto her? And what *is* your attitude toward the thief on the cross? Do you rejoice that, although he waited until the very last minutes of his life, that thief finally received Christ as Lord and Savior and thereby was granted entry into God's kingdom? Or does that bother you? Does it feel unfair to you that some people spend their entire lives in sinful rebellion against God and then, literally on their death beds or in a fox hole or on a cross, they come to saving faith in Christ, and instantaneously, they are forgiven, washed clean, and ushered into God's presence when they die? If so, you are the twelve-hour laborer. And God has a direct question for you: "Is your eye envious because I am generous?" (v. 15). In other words, do you resent my grace toward those who you deem unworthy, or at least less worthy than you?

Notice how the twelve-hour laborers vocalize their resentment toward the landowner: "… you have made them equal to us," referring to those who worked far less than they. Jesus, of course, included this particular grievance intentionally. By paying each of the workers the same exact wage, the landowner is indeed making them all equal. This is a picture of our salvation and of God's grace. Remember, we are saved by grace and not by works. Jesus makes this abundantly clear; whether you've worked twelve hours or just one hour, it's all the same wage. Why? Because salvation is not *at all* predicated on our labor but rather all on God's grace. Therefore, the time clock is totally irrelevant.

Taking this principle one step further, how exactly are we all made equal? And how could this possibly be fair?

The Bible teaches that we never really can produce a righteousness of our own through obedience to the law. But remember, God is righteous and holy, and He requires that same righteousness and holiness from anyone who desires to be in His presence. In Philippians 3, we read that the only righteousness that fits that bill is the imputed righteousness of Christ. We are clothed in the robes of *His* righteousness and thus are made worthy to abide in God's holy presence. In simplest terms, Christ's righteousness is what it is: perfect, whole, and complete. And He imparts it to all who believe and receive in equal portion. He imparts it fully. Therefore, all those who come to saving faith in the blood of Jesus Christ are made equally righteous. Everyone is fitted with the same robe! The imputed righteousness of Christ is the great equalizer.

> THE IMPUTED RIGHTEOUSNESS OF CHRIST IS THE GREAT EQUALIZER.

Do you understand this now? And are you hoping this is true? I encourage you, wherever you are at this moment, to bow your head and ask God to reveal the truth of His abundant grace to you. If you have been, as I was for most of my adult life, the twelve-hour laborer, grumbling against the landowner because of His generosity toward the late arrivers, ask Him to forgive you and set your heart straight. He will, and you will never be the same.

Reverend D.T. Niles once said, "Evangelism is witness. It is one beggar telling another beggar where to get food." I love that. It rings true to me. And it reflects our true position before God: we are all sinners saved by grace!

This strikes at the very heart of legalistic religion in general and at Mormonism specifically. Obedience to the "laws and ordinances of the gospel," even if that obedience is legitimate and well-intentioned, creates the illusion of worthiness. It sets one up for a false sense of superiority and favor with God. It also tends to promote a judgmental attitude toward those who are not as good at obeying God. In short, the legalist almost always becomes the twelve-hour laborer who resents the one-hour laborer and, ultimately, the landowner Himself. This is dangerous ground.

Peter has some excellent advice for those who have the tendency to get caught up in proving their worthiness to God, expecting more than one denarius for their efforts. First Peter 1:13 reads, "… fix yourself completely on the grace to be brought to you at the revelation of Jesus Christ." When we are focused exclusively on God's grace and our desperate need for that grace, there is no room for grumbling, resentment, or judgment. And when we hear of people who turn their lives around, no matter how late in the game, we genuinely rejoice in their salvation. Anything less than this puts the self-righteous legalist in the crosshairs of one of God's greatest ironies: "So the last shall be first, and the first last" (v. 16).

No one likes coming in last place. But as lousy as that might feel, the consequences are far more serious for the religionist who insists on adding something, anything, to God's grace as the basis for salvation. As it turns out, this concept of mixing grace with works/obedience as our means of salvation is nothing new. The early apostles had to deal with this very same teaching shortly after the establishment of Christ's church.

CHAPTER 15

THE JUDAIZERS (AND MODERN-DAY MORMONS)

> "Nor do people put new wine into old wineskins; otherwise the wineskins burst ..."
>
> —Matthew 9:17

Many Jews in and around Jerusalem came to recognize Jesus as Messiah and gladly laid aside all of their previous notions of righteousness under the Law in order to follow Him. Some were convinced by being witnesses to his miracles. Others, like the woman at the well, were converted through a single encounter with Him. And still others, like Peter, John, and Nathaniel, were hand chosen to be special disciples and witnesses to His divinity.

But there were other Jews who came to faith in Christ as Messiah who did not fully grasp the concept of salvation by grace or the idea that in Christ, the Law of Moses had been fulfilled. What they taught was a hybrid, a mixture of these two things; they taught grace plus works/obedience. We call these men Judaizers, and we are first introduced to them in Acts 15:1, which reads, "Some men came down from Judea and began teaching the brethren, 'Unless you are circumcised according to the custom of Moses, you cannot be saved.'"

It is not surprising that many of these Judaizers were Pharisees prior to their "conversion" to Christ. Their deeply rooted traditions of legalistic righteousness had conditioned them to hold on to the idea that, although

Jesus died to make atonement for their sins, they still had to obey the law in order to qualify for that gift. Does that sound familiar? Is this not precisely what the Latter-day Saints teach today? Yes, indeed.

In Acts 15:5 we read, "But some of the sect of the Pharisees who had believed stood up, saying, 'It is necessary to circumcise them and to direct them to observe the Law of Moses.'" Here, the Judaizers were specifically referring to converted Gentiles who never had been circumcised, let alone observed the Law of Moses. It was as if they were saying that in order to become a Christian, one must become a good Jew first. This, of course, made no sense to the true followers of Christ.

Peter, assuming the role of spokesman for the true followers, stepped in to correct this heresy: "Now therefore why do you put God to the test by placing upon the neck of the disciples a yoke which neither our fathers nor we have been able to bear? But we believe that we are saved through the grace of the Lord Jesus, in the same way as they also are" (Acts 15:10–11).

What Peter was saying, in essence, was this: "You have *got* to be kidding me! You claim to have come to faith in Christ as Lord and Savior, and yet you would have us all revert back to the Law? Christ clearly has provided a whole new way to the Father; in fact, He *is* the way! Yet you prefer the old way, which none of us were very good at to begin with. Did you somehow miss the part where He said, 'Whoever *believes* in [Me] will have eternal life' (Jn 3:15). What is wrong with you people?"

I find it interesting that this same debate continues to this very day and constitutes one of the fundamental impasses between the Christian and the devout Latter-day Saint. The Christian says to the Mormon, "I am saved by the grace of God based on my faith in Christ alone. There is nothing I can possibly do to earn my salvation. My salvation was purchased by the precious blood of Jesus on the cross, and my redemption was activated the moment I put my faith in His redeeming blood." The Christian might also add, "Now that I am saved, I want to live a life that honors and glorifies God. Any good works or obedience to God flows from a place of gratitude within me for what Christ already did for me."

The Mormon responds with, "Look, there is no way that salvation, eternal life in God's presence, could be that easy. Why would simple faith in Jesus qualify someone to receive all of God's riches, to be a co-inheritor with Christ? There's got to be more to it. Yes, Christ suffered and died for our sins, and it is only through the shed blood of Jesus that we can be forgiven. But we still have to obey God's commandments to be saved. We still have to be baptized and receive the gift of the Holy Ghost by the laying on of hands. We still have to attend our church meetings and pay tithing and not contaminate our bodies with tobacco or alcohol."

And if the Mormon really wanted to get down to particulars with his Christian friend, he would have to admit that, in order to live forever in the presence of God the Father (the equivalent of heaven to the Christian, making it an apples-to-apples comparison), one must also: fast once a month and donate a generous fast offering; take out one's endowment in the temple and then attend the temple regularly thereafter to perform this and other ordinances for the deceased; faithfully wear the garments of the holy priesthood; accept and magnify one's calling in the ward or stake; research one's family history (see temple work above); always be honest in one's dealings; do monthly home or visiting teaching; avoid gossip; avoid lustful thoughts; avoid contact with LDS apostates (oops, you're reading this book!); maintain a testimony of the Book of Mormon, Joseph Smith, and the Church of Jesus Christ of Latter-day Saints as the one true church; and on and on it goes.

Mormons are modern-day Galatians, influenced by the Judaizers. Exaltation and eternal life, according to LDS doctrine, is a combination of Christ's atoning sacrifice, *plus* obedience to the laws and ordinances of the gospel (see third Article of Faith). There is simply no way around this diagnosis.

Chuck the Janitor

Even so, for many years, I defended Mormonism as a legitimate iteration of Christianity. Mormons believe Jesus is the Son of God and that He died for our sins and rose again from the tomb. That was good enough for me. I figured that when my parents or my best friends passed on from this life, our loving God would simply strip away all of the superfluous religious stuff from their core Christianity, and presto, they would all enter into heaven's gates. In fact, a couple years ago, I wrote an essay—an allegory, really—with the purpose of defending Mormons as "good people" based on their excellent behavior. I called this allegory *Chuck the Janitor.*

Here's the basic story: Chuck is a hard-working young man who lands a job as a janitor with IBM in the early 1960s. In short order, he proves himself to be the hardest working, most diligent janitor the company has ever seen. Within two years, Chuck is promoted to be the head supervisor over all janitorial services at the main IBM campus. With this promotion comes a sizable pay raise.

One day, a major piece of machinery in one of the manufacturing plants breaks down. Before maintenance can even respond, Chuck jumps right in and fixes the machine! His superiors are so impressed with Chuck that he lands another promotion, this time as head of maintenance.

Right around this time, Chuck begins to reflect on his meteoric rise within the IBM Corporation. He begins to dream and dream big. Chuck sets for himself the goal of someday becoming President and CEO of IBM. With hard work and dedication, he knows he can do it. Look how far he's come already in just a few short years.

Chuck shares this dream only with his wife. Not wanting to hurt his feelings, she just smiles and encourages him to pursue his dreams. Secretly, she knows that without any formal education or training in business management, there is just no way that her husband is ever going to ascend to that level. But she loves Chuck and admires his drive.

Over the next thirty years, Chuck, through his amazing dedication and work ethic, continues to ascend the ranks at IBM. From head of maintenance, he moves on to foreman of one of the manufacturing plants. After running the tightest ship in the entire company, he eventually is named Senior Vice President over manufacturing! Chuck, now in his sixties, sees that he is just one small step away from being president. He commits to working harder than ever to make this a reality.

But ultimately, after forty years with IBM, the day comes for Chuck to retire. He never does become President and CEO, and he never was seriously considered by the board for that role, seeing that he had no formal education or business training. At no point was Chuck ever on track to be president. But the fact that *he* thought he could do it was what motivated him all those years to be such an excellent, diligent worker.

The devout Latter-day Saint believes that his ultimate destiny is to become "as God" (using the new, softened verbiage of current LDS publications), that someday, through eternal progression, he will rule and reign over his own creation and be a god worshipped by his own spirit children. As blasphemous as this may seem to the evangelical Christian, the question is: if this belief is what motivates the Mormon to live an upright, honest, sin-averse life, is that the worst thing in the world? Can't we as Christians just accept that, for the most part, Latter-day Saints live good, moral lives and just cut them some slack in terms of the underlying motivation for their morality? With all the evil in this world, is this really worth nitpicking?

For years, I didn't think it was. And then I read and finally grasped the significance of Paul's letter to the Galatians. My life would never be the same, and the purpose for my life, as it relates to reaching out to Latter-day Saints, became crystal clear.

You Foolish Galatians

Again, for those of you who have a Bible handy, take a few minutes to read Galatians from beginning to end. It's not a long letter and should take less than a half hour to read. For those that do not have a Bible on hand, let me briefly walk you through it, looking at the highlights of what Paul is urgently trying to convey to the saints in Galatia.

To give you some background, let me say that the very same Judaizers that we discussed earlier had made significant inroads among the early Christian converts of Galatia. Paul, who had planted the first church there, is writing this letter to combat the false teachings of the Judaizers, namely that salvation is achieved through faith in Christ, *plus* strict adherence to the Mosaic Law (including circumcision). This combination, according to the Judaizers, was the winning ticket. Paul, out of frustration and concern for these new (gullible) Christians, steps in to correct this heresy and defend the principle of justification by faith alone.

Paul's frustration is readily apparent from the outset: "I am amazed that you are so quickly deserting Him who called you by the grace of Christ, for a different gospel; which is really not another; only there are some who are disturbing you and want to distort the gospel of Christ" (Gal 1:6–8). Paul then goes on to say that if anyone, even he, were to come along and preach any gospel other than what he originally taught them, they should reject it out of hand. He then reasserts his authority as a messenger of the true gospel in verse 12: "For I neither received it from man, nor was I taught it, but I received it through a revelation of Jesus Christ." In other words, the gospel of grace that Paul taught came directly from Jesus Christ. Anything else, in this case a mixture of grace and works, is a distortion of the gospel and ought to be rejected.

In chapter 2, Paul reveals the underlying motivation of the Judaizers. Verse 4 says, "But it was because of the false brethren secretly brought in, who had sneaked in to spy out our liberty which we have in Christ Jesus, in order to bring us into bondage."

As they say, misery loves company. And in this case, the Judaizers just could not bear to see these new Christians enjoying freedom from the burdensome Law! Like crabs pulling their comrades back into the bucket, the Judaizers continually sought to pull their "brothers" back into bondage under the Law. So Paul reminds them that since Christ already fulfilled the Law and replaced it with a whole new gospel of grace predicated on faith (in Jesus), they were not to fall prey to this form of bondage. Galatians 2:16 reads, "Nevertheless knowing that a man is not justified by the works of the Law but through faith in Christ Jesus, even we have believed in Christ Jesus, so that we may be justified by faith in Christ and not by the works of the Law; since by the works of the Law no flesh will be justified."

> "... IF RIGHTEOUSNESS COMES THROUGH THE LAW, THEN CHRIST DIED NEEDLESSLY."

This is pretty straightforward language; it would be virtually impossible to misconstrue Paul's words here. We are not justified by the works of the Law but rather through faith in Christ. By the works of the Law absolutely no one will ever or could ever be justified and made right before a holy God—no one! Paul puts an emphatic exclamation mark on this point in verse 21: "... if righteousness comes through the Law, then Christ died needlessly."

At the beginning of chapter 3, it is obvious that the time for subtleties is over. Paul breaks out the sledgehammer. He writes, "You foolish Galatians! Who has bewitched you? Before your very eyes Jesus Christ was clearly portrayed as crucified. I would like to learn just one thing from you: Did you receive the Spirit by observing the law, or by believing what you heard? Are you so foolish? After beginning with the Spirit, are you now trying to attain your goal by human effort?" (Gal 3:1–3 NIV).

I still remember the first time I read this passage in the NIV. It was long after I left the LDS church. I remember thinking, "Boy, could anything better describe my experience as a Latter-day Saint?" Although I had begun with the Spirit, I was constantly seeking to please God and earn His favor through my own efforts—with very mixed results, I might add. It never occurred to me that the *work* of my salvation had already been completed. Anything short of an all-out effort to obey God's commandments and perform my duties in church felt like abject failure to me. Needless to say, because of my basic sin nature, I felt like a failure much of the time.

On a recent ski trip to Utah, I had the luxury of spending some quality time with my favorite uncle. He's the one who converted to Mormonism in 1955 and set into motion the events that ultimately led to my becoming LDS. As a matter of fact, he baptized me in 1974.

We got into a deep discussion late one night, and I was trying to describe to him what my "born-again" experience felt like and the ways in which my life had changed since my spiritual rebirth. His response reminded me of how little the average Latter-day Saint understands spiritual rebirth, as well as how much the focus remains on "human effort."

After listening to my story of how much I love God now, how much I want to live a life that honors Him, and how peaceful and secure I feel in my salvation, he responded with, "Well, John, your transformation is really just the culmination of a lot of preparation on your part. You've studied a lot. You've done a lot of good. It was just a matter of time." (He said something to that effect.)

And no matter how I tried to explain it, I just could not seem to convince him that, in reality, it was the exact *opposite* of what he was describing! It was only after I completely let go of my belief that I could somehow add to what Christ had done that I actually was filled with His Spirit and empowered to live for Him. This was precisely the distinction that Paul was trying to reestablish with the Galatians.

Paul spends the remainder of chapter 3 reminding the saints that it wasn't always about the Law. God's original covenant with Abraham was all about faith. Verse 6 says, "Even so Abraham believed God, and it was reckoned to him as righteousness." In verse 8, Paul explains that the Abrahamic Covenant was really a foreshadowing of grace, anticipating the day when, after the Law had run its course, "God would justify the Gentiles by faith."

No Longer Under a Tutor

So why did God institute the Law at all if we were all going to be justified by faith? We covered this in Chapter 6 of this book, but I believe it bears repeating. Apparently, Paul felt the need to remind the Galatians of this as well: "But before faith came, we were kept in custody under the Law, being shut up to the faith which was later to be revealed. Therefore the Law has become our tutor to lead us to Christ, so that we may be justified by faith. But now that faith has come, we are no longer under a tutor. For you are all sons of God through faith in Jesus Christ" (Gal 3:23–24).

What does it mean to say that the law "leads us to Christ?" Some (and probably most Mormons) would say that it is by our obedience to God's laws that we become more and more like Christ. And while there certainly is an element of truth to this, this is not what Paul is referring to. Remember, it was Paul who explained in his letter to the Romans: "For what the Law could not do, weak as it was through the flesh, God did; sending His own Son in the likeness of sinful flesh and as an offering for sin" (Ro 8:3). So, what Paul is getting at is that we simply cannot abide by every statute of the Law. We fail over and over again. At some point, the reasonable man throws up his hands, waves the little white flag, and gives up. "Lord, please save me!" he cries out. Bingo! These are the very words that lead us to Christ. And He does not come to us as a tutor, instructing us on how to be more like Him, at least not initially. He comes to save us as only He can.

In Chapter 4, Paul comes back to the theme of how our spiritual regeneration is, in reality, an adoption into the family of God. We become adopted sons and daughters of the Father the moment we place our trust in Christ. And from this moment forward, we enjoy intimate fellowship with the Father because of this new familial relationship. Paul once again points out to the Galatians how foolish it is to rescind this relationship and enter back into slavery under the Law. He states, "But now that you have come to know God, or rather to be known by God, how is it that you turn back again to the weak and worthless elemental things, to which you desire to be enslaved all over again? You observe days and months and seasons and years. I fear for you, that I have labored over you in vain" (Gal 4:9–11).

Paul had already made it clear that the Law was weak in that it was incapable of bringing about real and lasting spiritual rebirth. But now he adds that the Law is actually "worthless." And while this might have sounded brash to the Galatians, it should come as no surprise to us, dear reader. You'll remember that in our study of Philippians 3, Paul declared that all of his so-called qualifications as a Hebrew of Hebrews, including his impeccable righteousness under the Law, were but worthless "rubbish" compared to the surpassing value of knowing Christ and being found in Him (i.e., adopted into the family of God).

And yet here we see that the saints in Galatia had slipped back into observing certain customs, certain holidays from their old ways under the Law. And we know that they had readopted the practice of circumcision as an outward display of their righteousness before God. For Paul, the problem wasn't so much that they were doing these things. It was that they were attaching value, *salvation* value, to these things. Paul wonders out loud if everything he taught them had gone in one ear and out the other.

The letter to the Galatians reminds me of a boxing match. Paul is the undisputed heavyweight champion of the world. In chapters 1 through 4, Paul is jabbing away, exhausting his opponent, working the body, as they say. But the whole time, he's setting the Galatians up for the knock-out punch. That knock-out punch is Galatians 5:2–4. It reads: "Behold I, Paul, say to you that if you receive circumcision, Christ will be of no benefit to you. And I testify again to every man who receives circumcision that he is under obligation to keep the whole Law. You have been severed from Christ, you who are seeking to be justified by law; you have fallen from grace."

Paul says they *have been severed from Christ.* In this one brief passage, Paul exposes the danger and the consequences of seeking to be "justified by the law." And with this one clear warning, Paul puts the saints in Galatia on notice: Stop trying to mix grace and works, or you will lose the benefits of

Christ as your advocate when the day of judgment comes. You want to try your hand at being justified by the Law? Okay, have it your way. You will answer to the Law in that day. You will no longer be shielded from judgment by God's grace. Lots of luck with that!

But isn't Paul being a little harsh here? If I choose to be circumcised, I am severed from Christ? No, it's not about circumcision, per se. In fact, Paul clarifies in verse 6 that circumcision, in and of itself, is totally meaningless. It's when we attach meaning or value to circumcision, or to any of our outward works of obedience, that we offend God and sever ourselves from His grace. Why is this? Because the gospel of grace is predicated solely upon the completed work of Christ on the cross; He shed His blood for our salvation. "It is finished," He declared. As it turns out, the most consequential irony of them all is that we must accept that our debt to God was paid in full or we will pay the ultimate price: separation from His grace. And when we are separated from His grace, there is only one other way by which we could ever enter into God's kingdom—perfect obedience to God's law. That's a tall order indeed.

THE MOST CONSEQUENTIAL IRONY OF THEM ALL IS THAT WE MUST ACCEPT THAT OUR DEBT TO GOD WAS PAID IN FULL OR WE WILL PAY THE ULTIMATE PRICE.

CHAPTER 16

WITH APOLOGIES TO NEPHI

"But speaking the truth in love, we are to grow up in all aspects into Him who is the head, even Christ …"

—Ephesians 4:15

Now, let's put Paul and the Galatians on the shelf for a minute. I want to speak directly to you, my LDS reader. But I will warn you up front that this might be a little uncomfortable. You probably won't like what I am about to tell you. You might even hate me for it. And that's okay. My love for you exceeds my fear of you hating me. Perfect love, after all, casts out all fear (1 Jn 4:8). And although my love may not be perfect, it's just going to have to do for now.

So here it goes. Modern-day Mormons are the Galatians of old. Joseph Smith; Brigham Young; and every "prophet, seer, and revelator" on down, they all are the Judaizers who have distorted the true gospel of Jesus Christ. And for any Latter-day Saint in particular, the degree to which you are seeking to be justified by law, in other words, proving your worthiness to live with Heavenly Father someday, is the degree to which you have fallen from grace.

Every time you go to church or attend the temple, every time you pay tithing or fast offerings, every time you help someone in need and think that you're winning points with God or in any way contributing to your own salvation, you are severed from Christ. Every time you magnify your calling as a primary teacher or write in your journal or send a care package to a full-time missionary and think that these things impress God and help you to any degree at all in your quest to end up in the celestial kingdom, you put yourself in the position where Christ will be of no benefit to you. And if every time you resist the urge to view online pornography, smoke a cigarette, or tell a lie to save face with someone you feel more worthy to enter into God's presence, you are literally fallen from grace. Christ will not be your advocate before the Father. You will be on your own, held accountable to the Law. And if you are anything like every other person who has tried this approach, you will perish. This is what God tells us in His Word.

I beg of you, stop trying to prove your worthiness to God. Admit, first to yourself and then to God, that in reality you prove your *un*worthiness to Him every day of your life. We all do. There is only one who is worthy, and that is Jesus Christ. We have one responsibility in our own salvation: to believe in Jesus' redeeming blood shed on the cross and to receive the grace that this blood produced. Nothing less, but equally important, nothing *more* will secure our salvation. Please understand that trying to add to God's grace negates His grace. I know this is counter-intuitive. I know this runs totally against everything you've ever been taught. But do you have the faith to not only believe *in* Christ but also to *believe* Christ when He says that the work of your salvation was already completed? Any effort to contribute to your salvation is tantamount to telling Christ that His sacrifice was not enough, that His blood was insufficient.

Would you ever consider adding your own finishing touches to DaVinci's *Mona Lisa* (assuming you could get past security)? How about Mozart's *Symphony No. 40* in G minor? Surely you could improve on that work—add a little here and there to sort of spice it up a bit. Hey, I know. Why don't you give Michael Jordan some pointers on how to play basketball? Not in a million years.

Jesus Christ suffering and dying on the cross *is* God's great masterpiece. It is the central event in human history and the Father's ultimate display of His awesome love. Christ's sacrifice is perfect, exactly as it is. We don't add to it; we don't subtract from it; we don't alter it; and we don't question its perfection, sufficiency, or simplicity. Paul wrote to the saints in Corinth: "But I fear, lest by any means, as the serpent

JESUS CHRIST SUFFERING AND DYING ON THE CROSS *IS* GOD'S GREAT MASTERPIECE.

beguiled Eve through his subtlety, so your minds should be corrupted from the *simplicity that is in Christ*" (2 Cor 11:3 KJV, italics mine). And yet far too many religions, with Mormonism perhaps being the poster child, do just that.

How do I know this is what Mormonism espouses? Because it's everywhere. It permeates virtually every Sunday school lesson, every General Conference talk, and every missionary discussion. And it isn't just Mormon culture; it's Mormon doctrine. Any Latter-day Saint worth his salt knows 2 Nephi 25:23 by heart: "… for we know that it is by grace that we are saved, after all we can do."

Actually, Nephi, according to the Bible, we are saved by grace only when we admit that there is *nothing* we can do except put our full faith and trust in Christ. Once again, dear LDS reader, you have to decide whether Nephi is right or Paul is right. They cannot both be right, and you cannot afford to be wrong. Your eternal life depends on it.

And finally, the most obvious evidence that Mormonism is a modern-day distortion of the true gospel, in the same tradition as the Judaizers of old, is the LDS third Article of Faith: "We believe that through the Atonement of Christ, all mankind may be saved, by obedience to the laws and ordinances of the Gospel."

Maybe if Joseph Smith had put a period after the word "saved" rather than a comma, we wouldn't be having this conversation. I probably would never have had any inclination to write this book. But what follows the comma, to most Christians, categorizes the Mormon religion as a legalistic, quasi-Christian entity at best. More importantly, it is what severs the devout Latter-day Saint from the grace of God. (I told you this would be uncomfortable.)

To the Latter-day Saint, this is *beyond* uncomfortable. You may be thinking, *You're telling me that the very* thought *that my obedience and good works are contributing to my salvation severs me from God's grace? Nonsense! This strains logic and does not at all square with my concept of a loving, gracious God. This is just way too extreme!*

To which I would respond, "Yes, it *is* extreme!" But so was the extreme suffering of Jesus on the cross. And so are the extremely lavish riches of living in perfect joy with God in His kingdom someday. And so was the declaration by Jesus Himself when He said, "Narrow is the way that leads to eternal life and few there are that find it. Broad is the way that leads to destruction …" Extreme, extreme, extreme.

There's an old Chinese proverb that says, "When you pick up one end of the stick, you pick up the other." And I believe that's what we have here.

God's gift of eternal life is extreme in its wonderfulness. God's chosen method of redemption to provide this gift is extreme in its simplicity—"the simplicity of the cross." (Remember, this very message was vehemently opposed by the religious leaders in Jesus' day. They killed Him for it!)

This is not to say that Mormons are alone in this error of the Judaizers, not by any stretch. Christians are often just as guilty of striving to earn their salvation. Theologian John H. Shelton writes:

> So the error of the Judaizers is both a modern error as well as a very ancient error. It is found in the modern church wherever men seek salvation by "surrender" instead of by faith, or by their own character instead of by the imputed righteousness of Christ, or by "making Christ master in my life" instead of trusting in the redeeming blood. It is found wherever men say that the real essentials of Christianity are love, justice, mercy, and other virtues, as contrasted with the great doctrines of God's word. These are all just different ways of exalting the merit of man over the cross of Christ.
>
> —*Notes on Galatians*, p. 10

For me, it has been a process. When I was LDS, I attributed approximately half of my salvation to what Christ did for me and the other half to my obedience to God's commandments, performance of certain ordinances, and acts of service to others—give or take a few percentage points. When I first started attending church in a non-denominational Christian setting, I dumped the ordinances altogether and assigned those points over onto the Jesus side. So by about 2002 or so, I saw my salvation as about 70 percent Jesus to 30 percent John.

Then a few things happened to me on my way to living out my days in the 70 to 30 range. Sometime in the spring of 2003, I went to see *The Passion of the Christ* on the big screen. I walked out of that theater a changed man. And as painful as it is for me to admit even now, I acknowledge that until I saw *The Passion*, I never really loved Jesus. I never really felt a profound gratitude for what He did for me. I had only paid lip service to His role as Savior in my life. Now I was ready to change the ratio to 80 percent Jesus, 20 percent John. Boy, He really earned that additional 10 percent!

Then, in 2004, I was completely broken, in every sense of the word, by a devastating divorce from the only woman I had ever loved. I couldn't sleep. I couldn't eat. And if it weren't for my son and the love I had for him, I don't know what would have become of me. But as it turns out, it took *that* level of brokenness in me to finally get me to admit that I was completely and utterly helpless in this world without the Lord.

In that brokenness, I determined to really seek God. For the first time in my life, I spent a significant amount of time on my knees in prayer. But this was prayer like I had never known before. This was desperate prayer. This was, "Lord, please just be here with me. Let me know you're there. I need you, and I can't make it through this day without you! Lead me into the light and show me who you want me to be." I was literally living one hour at a time.

I bought a new Bible during that time, one that was more understandable to me. And I determined to study the Bible with the sole purpose of drawing closer to God. No longer was I interested in studying the Bible to determine which religion I should belong to. I didn't necessarily see it as a scholarly endeavor. I wasn't doing it because it was a commandment. The best way I can describe it is that I felt compelled, magnetically drawn to God's Word. I remember racing home every day after work just to get back to the Bible. I focused on the New Testament primarily, and in so doing, I found that the "good news of the gospel," the gospel of grace, was beginning to come alive in me. Day after day, chapter after chapter, the central theme of the New Testament was sinking in deeper: It's not about me; it's all about the cross of Jesus! He did it all. Even so, almost inexplicably, I still held on to about 1 percent of the responsibility for my salvation. So for another six years or so, I shuffled along at 99 percent Jesus, 1 percent John.

I was hedging my bets. My thought process was, *I'm pretty sure Jesus purchased my salvation when He died on the cross. But just in case there is some truth to the religious concept that I need to do my part, I'm going to go ahead and be in church every Sunday, pay tithing, and do nice things for people just because.* I was still assigning value to my acts of righteousness. My prideful ego just could not let go of that last little vestige of hope that what I was doing mattered.

As it turns out, there was a reason I couldn't let go of that 1 percent. I had not yet been born again of God's Spirit! Despite all my studies, church attendance, acts of service, Bible knowledge, faith sharing, and prayer, I had not yet "died to self" and become a "new creation in Christ." The moment I let go of self and received Christ fully, I knew I had crossed over to 100:0. And for the first time in my entire life, I had total peace. It was September, 2010.

Deconstructing James

Brigham Young is quoted as saying, "Pray as though everything depended on the Lord and work as though everything depended on you." I can't think of a quote that better exemplifies the Mormon mindset. Most Latter-day Saints I know take pride in this ethic, this perceived partnership between God and man. God did His part, and we've got to do ours.

Interestingly, I've noticed that whenever the topic of salvation by faith vs. salvation by faith plus works comes up, the Mormon almost always turns to the Bible (of all places) to prove that faith alone is insufficient. And without fail, the same three scriptures emerge. The first is Matthew 5:48, which reads, "Be ye therefore perfect, even as your Father in heaven is perfect." The second is Philippians 2:12, which reads, in part, "… work out your salvation with fear and trembling." And the third is, of course, the second chapter of James, where it says, "Faith without works is dead." For sake of space and time, I would like to focus our attention on James 2.

Admittedly, at first glance, James seems to be contradicting the teachings of Paul. In fact, let's read two verses back-to-back, one from Paul and one from James. Then I'll take my best stab at reconciling these two passages for my LDS friends.

You've probably already noticed that one of the linchpin verses supporting the central theme of this book is Ephesians 2:8–9. Paul writes, "For it is by grace you have been saved *through faith*; and that not of yourselves, it is the gift of God; *not as a result of works*, so that no one may boast" (italics mine).

But then we flip back a few pages and read another verse, one from no less of an authority than James, the half-brother of Jesus. James 2:24 says, "You see that a man is *justified by works* and *not by faith alone*" (italics mine).

Now, most Latter-day Saints who are experienced in apologetics will, when discussing these two passages, seek to score a "double whammy" with their evangelical friends. First, they will point to James 2:24 to support their view of salvation as being a product of faith *and* works. It appears to be pretty clear language, after all. Then second, they will often seek to use these two seemingly contradictory passages as proof that the Bible is unreliable and only worthy of our serious attention when it is "translated correctly." Sadly, according to them, the Bible is rarely (if ever) translated correctly, and these two verses are their "Exhibits A and B."

But are these two passages really contradictory? Or is it possible that in the larger context, the writings of Paul and James work together to describe not only the process of salvation but also how that salvation (born-again experience) manifests itself in the life of the true believer? Any honest and thorough study of the New Testament reveals that the latter is true. So let's look at James 2 together. It's a perfect way to close out this chapter and usher us into the next section.

James launches into this subject with a very fair question: "What use is it, my brethren, if someone says he has faith but he has no works? Can that faith save him?" (Jas 2:14). Then James answers his own question with a hypothetical situation. What if someone is without adequate food and clothing, and he or she comes to you for help? Can you just say to that person, "Go in peace, be warmed and be filled" and expect that to help with his or her physical needs? James asks, "What use is that?" (v. 16). Tying this back in with his point, James explains, "Even so faith, if it has no works, is dead, being by itself" (v. 17).

There's absolutely no argument here. Martin Luther once said, "We are saved by faith alone, but saving faith is never alone." It is always accompanied by good works! James had already hinted at this dynamic in chapter 1. In fact, he was simply echoing Jesus' exact same teaching on this when he wrote the following: "But prove yourselves doers of the word, and not merely hearers who delude themselves" (Jas 1:22).

The doing of the Word does not save us; our faith does. But our doing provides outward, verifiable evidence of our inner, unseen faith. And it is this very outward proof of inner faith that James is driving at in James 2:18: "But someone may well say, 'You have faith and I have works; show me your faith without works, and I will show you my faith by my works.'"

OUR DOING PROVIDES OUTWARD, VERIFIABLE EVIDENCE OF OUR INNER, UNSEEN FAITH.

I'm a dentist. I spent approximately ten years in training (college and dental school), and I've been practicing dentistry for twenty years. So, for the last thirty years, I've acquired knowledge and developed skills that allow me to successfully correct a person's dental problems. I am not, however, a dentist because I fix people's teeth. I fix people's teeth because I am a dentist! Does that make sense? In other words, in about three hours, I could train a carpenter (someone who is good with his hands) to place a filling in someone's molar. Does that make him a dentist? No, it does not. On the other hand, I could bring in a dentist from virtually anywhere in the world, and he would already know how to fill that molar—because he is a dentist.

By the same token, I am not a Christian because I do good works. Rather, I do good works because I am a Christian.

Another thing to consider is that works do not necessarily imply faith. The world is full of wonderful, kind, highly moral individuals who are committed atheists. Their good works do nothing to help them on judgment day if they do not have faith in Jesus Christ. So, I guess in an inversion of James's argument, we see that works without faith are dead too!

Next James strides confidently into his closing argument, and he uses two wildly different examples to prove his point: the belief of the demons and the justification of Abraham.

In verse 19, James offers this chilling reminder. "You believe that God is one. You do well; the demons also believe, and shudder." So the demons believe in Jesus. They even believe that He is the Son of God and that He died for the sins of the world! But this belief, this faith in Jesus does not save them. Why? Because it's not *saving faith*. They were never born again of God's Spirit, nor will they ever be. They never received Christ as Lord and Savior. And James's over-arching point here regarding the demons is that their faith is not saving faith because they have no outward works to substantiate the kind of faith that saves. And so it is with every so-called Christian.

I know that Latter-day Saints really struggle with the person who claims to be Christian, claims to be saved by grace and going to heaven, but just carries on living a life of overt sinfulness and rebellion against God's commandments. Trust me, the mature Christian has the same concern for this person! We might even say, depending on the case, that the person living this way is being led by the flesh and not by God's Spirit and was likely never saved to begin with. And we arrive at this conclusion from what the Bible teaches. Paul writes:

> For the flesh sets its desire against the Spirit … Now the deeds of the flesh are evident, which are: immorality, impurity, sensuality, idolatry, sorcery, enmities, strife, jealousy, outbursts of anger, disputes, dissensions, factions, envying, drunkenness, carousing, and things like these, of which I forewarn you, just as I have forewarned you, that *those that practice such things will not inherit the kingdom of God.*
>
> —Galatians 5:17–20, italics mine

So, let's dispense of this notion of "easy grace" right now. No teacher of the Bible would ever defend a "believer" whose life looked anything like what Paul described above.

We are going to dig deeper into what it means to live the Christian life in the next section. But for now, suffice to say, true, saving faith is always accompanied by good works and obedience to God's commandments. And who better to use as an example of this winning combination than Father Abraham. In James 2:21–24, we read:

> Was not Abraham our father justified by works when he offered up Isaac his son on the altar? You see that faith was working with his works, and as a result of the works, faith was perfected; and the scripture was fulfilled which says, "And Abraham believed God, and it was reckoned to him as righteousness," and he was called the friend of God. You see that a man is justified by works and not by faith alone.

This is meaty, and there's a little something for everyone here. James starts off by saying that Abraham was "justified by works" when he showed his willingness to plunge a dagger into his beloved son Isaac. But let's face it; even though the physical act of sacrificing one's own son is technically an outward work, it really is a test of a man's faith! This is why James immediately draws our attention to how faith and works are "working together." In other words, in passing the ultimate test of faith by this act of obedience (work), Abraham's faith was "perfected."

Now we come full circle, to what seemed to be a contradictory claim found in verse 24: "You see that a man is justified by works and not faith alone." This is a statement to which both Mormons and Christians can say, "Amen!" Faith without works is dead.

So, it is not:

FAITH + WORKS = SALVATION

Rather, it's:

FAITH (THAT WORKS) = SALVATION

Conclusion

So now we see the danger of trying to mix God's grace with our works—it undoes everything. Works, in and of themselves, are good. But when we assign value to them and believe that they are even partially responsible for our salvation, we run into trouble. We are severed from grace and on our own to try to elevate ourselves to worthiness, which is impossible. This is why we must put *all* (100 percent) of our trust in the completed work of our salvation at the cross of Jesus. It is *paid in full.* There's nothing left to pay, even if we wanted to. In fact, the suffering of Christ on the cross is the very reason why the Father can be so gracious. His wrath was exhausted on His Son—for all those who belong to Him.

It's like your team winning the Super Bowl and you accepting a trophy and a championship ring, even though you were a fifth-string offensive lineman and never played a snap all season long, not even in pre-season! But you're on the winning team. You wear that jersey just as proudly as the star quarterback. You are a champion because you belong to the championship team, and no one can take that ring away from you.

Belonging to Christ, putting our full faith and trust in His redeeming blood, believing that His suffering and death paid for our sins and made us worthy before a holy God, places us on the winning team. This *is* our salvation, and there is no other way. Jesus said, "I am the way, the truth, and the life; no one comes to the Father but through Me" (Jn 14:6). He didn't say, "I know the way. I know the truth. I know how you can live." He *is* the way. Any other way, including our arrogant attempts at proving our worthiness, is a dead end.

Let's spend some time now looking at what it means to be "born again" and to live the Christian life. Let's find out how faith works.

SECTION VI
A NEW CREATION

CHAPTER 17

BORN AGAIN

Behold, I make all things new …

—Revelation 21:5

In the fall of 1989, my former wife and I left the shadows of the Wasatch Front. I had just graduated from BYU in the spring and was making the trek to Los Angeles to start dental school at UCLA.

UCLA was quite a culture shock for me, coming from the immaculate, well-behaved confines of Brigham Young University to the … (hmm, how do I put this?) … to the rowdy, alcohol-soaked environment of UCLA. *This is grad school?* I did have five LDS classmates, but the majority of the other eighty-seven were, let's just say, not nearly as committed to the Word of Wisdom as we were.

My classmates, as it turned out, were fantastic, and I had a very positive experience at UCLA. But one of my classmates was decidedly different from the rest of us. His name was Ethan; although, some of my classmates called him Jesus because of his peaceful demeanor and really cool beard.

Ethan was quiet but not necessarily shy. He was serene, in a comfortable, self-assured sort of way. And he was gracious and kind, not just sometimes—always. I cannot remember a single occasion when he spoke an unkind or critical word to anyone about anything. He was also very humble, despite being an excellent student and very capable clinician. Ethan was special, and I knew it—and it really bothered me. It bothered me because, as our four-year association progressed, I discovered that Ethan was special in all the ways that I should have been special but wasn't. Ethan was a born-again Christian.

Ethan and I spent hundreds (if not thousands) of hours talking over those years. He and his wife lived right upstairs from us in student housing, and we rode the bus to and from Westwood together nearly every day. He was quite knowledgeable about Mormon doctrine and practices, and yet I knew next to nothing about what made him tick. I remember being baffled when I asked, "What religion do you belong to?"

"I don't belong to any religious denomination," he responded.

I don't believe he ever mentioned what church he attended; if he did, it certainly was never a point of emphasis.

"I'm a follower of Jesus," he said.

"Well, sure, so am I," I responded. "I belong to the Church of Jesus Christ of Latter-day Saints! It says His name right there in the middle." The fact is, only one of us was a true follower of Jesus at that time, and I was not the one.

To me, before I met Ethan, a born-again Christian was someone who wanted to take the easy road. It's all about Jesus—Jesus, Jesus, Jesus. They'd say things like, "I am saved by grace because of what Jesus did for me on the cross. And since I know I'm going to heaven, I don't want to be bothered with rules and commandments. I go to church, but I don't *have* to. I pay tithes to my church but only because I *want* to; it's not a commandment (and it certainly isn't 10 percent of my income!). I drink wine, just not to excess. Basically, my salvation is secure because I don't live under the law but under grace." And my thought was always, *Well, isn't that convenient. If only it were that easy.*

But after I came to know Ethan, and after all the hair-splitting and doctrine comparing was exhausted, I was forced to confront a whole set of undeniable facts. Ethan was uncompromising in his faith, and I made compromises left and right. Ethan was supremely confident in his salvation, and I was constantly seeking to prove to God that I was good enough, yet never really knowing if I made the grade. Ethan was at peace; I was in turmoil. Like Nicodemus of old, I was left wondering, "How can these things be?"

Born of the Spirit

Remember, it was Nicodemus, a Pharisee and teacher of Israel, who came to Jesus in the middle of the night, seeking wisdom from someone he considered to be a master teacher of the Law. But Jesus wasn't interested in discussing the Law; He cut right to the heart of the matter and said to Nicodemus, "Truly, truly I say to you, unless one is born again he cannot see the kingdom of God" (Jn 3:3).

Jesus then went on to distinguish between being born of the flesh (physical birth from one's mother) and being "born of the Spirit" (a spiritual rebirth every bit as real and necessary as physical birth). He then compared this spiritual rebirth to the wind: "The wind blows where it wishes and you hear the sound of it, but do not know where it comes from and where it is going; so is everyone who is born of the Spirit" (Jn 3:8).

What a curious comparison. What does Jesus mean by this? Clearly this is not a detailed, comprehensive explanation of how spiritual rebirth happens or even what it looks like. Jesus' point is that, like the wind blowing, it's mysterious. We don't really understand how God's Spirit works, but like the wind, we can feel and see the effect it has. People born again of God's Spirit are, in a word, changed and, in many cases, radically changed. Paul writes in 2 Corinthians 5:17: "Therefore if anyone is in Christ, he is a new creation; the old things passed away; behold, new things have come."

Elder Bruce R. McConkie, in *Mormon Doctrine*, explains what being "born again" means to the Latter-day Saints: "The second birth begins when men are baptized in water by a legal administrator; it is completed when they actually receive the companionship of the Holy Ghost ..." (*MD*, p. 101). Now, in all fairness to Elder McConkie, he does go on to say that mere compliance with these two ordinances does not guarantee the spiritual rebirth of any given individual. He adds, "The new birth takes place only for those who actually enjoy the gift or companionship of the Holy Ghost, only for those who are fully converted ..." (p. 101). This, presumably, would be a safeguard against anyone trying to fake his or her way to spiritual rebirth and then on into heaven. Fair enough.

But if the above view is what Jesus meant by being born again, why did He compare it to the wind blowing? Why does He leave Nicodemus with the idea that spiritual rebirth is ethereal, mysterious, and other-worldly? When Nicodemus asked Jesus point blank, "How can these things be?" wouldn't Jesus have simply responded with the two-step process of baptism by immersion and the gift of the Holy Ghost by the laying on of hands? Technically, if Nicodemus were open to it, couldn't Jesus have just done the job right then and there? He certainly had the authority.

This late-night interaction between Nicodemus and Jesus reminds me very much of my early morning conversations with Ethan years ago.

Unfortunately, I was Nicodemus. I was attached to laws, ordinances, and "legal administration," altogether unfamiliar with the Holy Spirit and this mysterious phenomenon of being "born again." As it turns out, I was not alone.

The Woman at the Well

In the very next chapter, the apostle John delves deeper into this mystery of spiritual rebirth by recording the conversation between Jesus and a Samaritan woman drawing water from a well. You would be hard pressed to draw a more stark contrast between the characters of chapters 3 and 4: Nicodemus, the highly respected, scholarly, and pious Pharisee and the Samaritan woman—not at all respected, uneducated, and apparently very worldly. Yet it seems John is trying to show us something: that regardless of our backgrounds, we are all equally desperate for what Jesus is offering. And what He is offering is nothing short of complete spiritual rebirth.

REGARDLESS OF OUR BACKGROUNDS, WE ARE ALL EQUALLY DESPERATE FOR WHAT JESUS IS OFFERING.

Nicodemus comes to Jesus in the middle of the night, presumably to avoid being found out by his colleagues. On the other hand, Jesus approaches the Samaritan woman under the hot sun of mid-day. Nicodemus comes to Jesus thinking he has, because of his mastery of the law, all the answers. His primary curiosity appears to be Jesus' miracles. The Samaritan woman is under no such illusion. She is simply waiting for Messiah, who, "when that one comes, He will declare all things to us" (Jn 4:25). And finally, Nicodemus thinks he has every right to approach Jesus because they are, in a sense, colleagues; both are "teachers of Israel." The Samaritan woman can't believe that Jesus is even talking to her, let alone asking her for a drink! Everyone knew that Jews had no dealings with Samaritans (v. 9). But Jesus isn't concerned about social norms. He came to save souls, and by His actions, He provides us with valuable insights into what He means by spiritual rebirth.

After the woman at the well expresses her shock at Jesus' requesting a cup of water from her, Jesus opens up the dialogue: "If you knew the gift of God, and who it is who says to you, 'Give me a drink,' you would have asked Him, and He would have given you *living water*" (Jn 4:10, italics mine).

Well, she likes the sound of this "living water" that Jesus speaks of but immediately puts limitations on His ability to provide it. "Sir, you have nothing to draw with and the well is deep." She does, however, manage to ask the right question of Jesus: "… where then do you get this living water?" (v. 11).

Jesus responds, "Everyone who drinks of this water will thirst again; but whoever drinks of the water that I will give him shall never thirst; but the water that I will give him will become in him a well of water springing up to eternal life" (Jn 4:13–14).

"Well, hey, lay some of that living water on me, brother, because I'm getting tired of having to come all the way down here every day to draw more!" I'm paraphrasing, but this is essentially her response. What she doesn't realize, not yet anyway, is that she has spoken the very words Jesus longed to hear: "Sir, give me this water …" (v. 15). And this is where it gets interesting, because although Jesus' response appears to come out of left field, He is actually responding to her request for living water.

Let's follow the fascinating dialogue found in verses 16–19:

> He said to her, "Go, call your husband and come here." The woman answered and said, "I have no husband." Jesus said to her, "You have correctly said, I have no husband, for you have had five husbands, and the one you now have is not your husband; this you have said truly." The woman said to Him, "Sir, I perceive that you are a prophet."

In short order, she perceived Him to be a whole lot more than just a prophet. In fact, she immediately, upon being informed of His true identity, accepted Jesus as Messiah and "Savior of the world" (v. 42). But for now, let's go back to His command that she go and get her husband. This command served to expose two facts: 1) She had already gone through five husbands. 2) She was currently living in sin with a man to whom she was not married. Even in Samaria, this was almost unheard of and certainly considered to be grossly immoral.

And this is the whole point. Jesus is saying if you want spiritual rebirth (to be born again as He described it to Nicodemus), if you want to never thirst (spiritually) again, if you want to receive a "well of water springing up to eternal life," you are going to have to confront your sin. There is no other way.

Remember, as we discussed in Chapter 5, sin is what separates us from a holy God. Sin is what disqualifies us from ever being able to abide in His presence. Therefore, sin keeps us out of heaven. It really is just that simple. Paul writes to the Corinthians: "The sting of death is sin, and the power of sin is the law; but thanks be to God, who gives us the victory through our Lord Jesus Christ" (1 Cor 15:56–57).

So, if receiving the living water that Christ offers (the equivalent of being born again of God's Spirit) is our way to eternal life, then this water must be the solution to the sin problem. Indeed it is, and here's why: Three things change the moment we receive Christ as Lord and Savior and are born again of God's Spirit (the first two are a review of what we've already discussed). First, our *legal* standing with God changes; we go from being condemned sinners and objects of His wrath to forgiven sinners, acquitted of all charges. Because Jesus absorbed the full penalty for our sins, we are no longer required to pay the penalty for those sins. We are declared righteous precisely because He was declared guilty and punished accordingly. This, if you recall, is the divine exchange. Second, our *relational* standing with God changes. We go from being strangers or, worse yet, rebels against God to adopted children of God, co-inheritors with Christ of all the Father has. And third, an *inherent* change occurs within us as the Holy Spirit literally comes in to dwell in our hearts, empowering us to live for God's purposes and to His glory. And it is to this inherent change, this well of living water, that we will devote the remainder of this chapter.

THEN THIS WATER MUST BE THE SOLUTION TO THE SIN PROBLEM. INDEED IT IS.

Dying to Live

Before we can talk about spiritual rebirth, however, we have to back up exactly one step and talk about death, in this case, death to self. Jesus said, "Truly, truly, I say to you, unless a grain of wheat falls into the earth and dies, it remains alone; but if it dies, it bears much fruit. He who loves his life loses it, and he who hates his life in this world will keep it to life eternal" (Jn 12:24–25). Jesus is primarily referring to Himself in this passage. Just as a kernel of wheat must die in the dry earth in order to germinate and bring forth a rich harvest, so must the Son of God die in order to bring about the salvation of many. But at the same time, He is referring to His followers as well. There comes that moment in every believer's life when he must be willing to die to self, die to his agenda, die to the lusts of his flesh, and ultimately, die to this world and everything in it. Paul writes to the Galatians: "But may it never be that I would boast, except in the cross of our Lord Jesus Christ, through which the world has been crucified to me, and I to the world" (Gal. 6:14).

This is not a one-time proposition. God fully intends for His children to live (and, paradoxically, to die) one day at a time. Paul wrote, "I die daily" (1 Cor 15:31). What Paul understood was that in order to live for God, he had to put to death his flesh—and then repeat this process every single day. Remember, we are all living, breathing contradictions; we are semi-functional "civil wars" of the spirit and the flesh. But Paul offers this encouragement (and warning) to the Galatians: "But I say, walk by the Spirit, and you will not carry out the desire of the flesh. For the flesh sets its desire against the Spirit, and the Spirit against the flesh; for these are in opposition to one another, so that you may not do the things that you please" (Gal. 5:17).

GOD FULLY INTENDS FOR HIS CHILDREN TO LIVE (AND, PARADOXICALLY, TO DIE) ONE DAY AT A TIME.

Which of these wins the battle? The simplest answer is: the one you feed. But Paul, echoing the teachings of Jesus, invites us to take it one step further—we are to "die daily." It will be difficult for our flesh to prevail if it's dead.

My Personal D-Day, November 6, 2004

Rarely does the believer experience death of self and spiritual rebirth in a single moment; although, it does happen. For me, it has come in waves. And when I reflect back on those moments in which the Lord has powerfully worked in my heart to change me and give me new life, I realize that He has been working with me one sin issue at a time. Let me get real personal with you for a minute as I describe the morning of November 6, 2004, for this was *the* turning point of my life.

Six weeks prior (September 27, 2004, to be exact), my wife of five years left me. No warning, just gone. She took the nice car, took most of the furnishings in our home, and split. I was devastated. In a matter of three weeks, I lost close to twenty-five pounds! I couldn't eat, couldn't sleep, and was barely able to function at work.

I remember getting to that point where I literally did not care whether I lived or died, and there was nothing I could do to pull myself up and out of that place. I was broken, completely and utterly shattered. Thank goodness! Because the fact is that I was a selfish, arrogant, money-addicted jerk! I say money, but what I really mean is wealth. I was obsessed with wealth and wealth building. My every thought, from the moment I awoke in the morning until my head hit the pillow at night, was about money and wealth: stock market, real estate, rehab properties, *Investors Business Daily*, *Wall Street Journal*, speculation, side businesses, and on and on it went. And that's not even counting my core career, which was dentistry.

The Bible says, "Do not love the world nor the things in the world. If anyone loves the world, the love of the Father is not in him" (1 Jn 2:15). Needless to say, the love of the Father was not in me. And if God's love was not in me, there was no way I was loving my wife the way I needed to. No wonder she left.

Six weeks later, on an overcast Saturday morning, the full weight of my own awfulness came crashing down on me like a tidal wave. I sat on the edge of my sofa, looked out over my virtually empty house, and began to sob. This was pain unlike anything I had ever experienced before, a deep anguish of soul. And I came to accept at that very moment that I was responsible for every bit of that anguish. I wept uncontrollably.

Somewhere in the weeping, God spoke clearly into my mind, *"John, your love for money and the things of this world has brought you to this place of brokenness."*

In a flash, I knew what to do. I cried out, literally out loud, "God, please take this away from me! I don't want to be this man anymore. Please, God, make me a new man! I don't want to love money anymore." And I *meant* it. There was nothing in me that resisted this cry, no internal conflict or double-mindedness. I hated who I had become (yet again) and desperately needed God to change me.

I do not pretend to have words adequate to describe what happened next. But instantaneously, I *knew* He had heard my cry. I knew that I had been changed. Like a flash of blinding light, He reached into my heart, removed my love for money, and replaced it with a love for His Word! As I mentioned before, I did the only thing I could think to do; I raced to the local Christian bookstore and bought a new Bible.

Anyone who knew me prior to November of 2004 will tell you that I am a radically different person since that day. In a moment, God heard my cry and healed my heart. And to this day, almost nine years later, I cannot even *make* myself love money or the things of this world. It is just not in me.

CHAPTER 18

ABIDE IN ME

Popular Bible teacher John Coursin once wrote, "The Christian race is the only race in the world that begins at the finish line. We don't fight *for* victory, we fight *from* victory. The battle's already won—Jesus overcame!"

Most Latter-day Saints that I talk to have a difficult time accepting the notion that Christ already purchased our salvation and that we can only receive it by faith as a gift from God. Moreover, the concept of imputed righteousness (imputed from Christ to us) runs entirely counter to the Mormon mindset, a mindset predicated on proving one's worthiness to God through obedience and good works.

This leads to another thing the Latter-day Saint struggles with: the perception of complacency on the part of those who insist they are saved by grace. If your salvation is "in the bag," what could possibly motivate you to be a good person and do good things? Wouldn't this just open the door for worldly living? I mean, if all your sins are covered by God's grace, why not just live it up? This was certainly my thought process when I was LDS. What it really demonstrated was my utter lack of understanding of what spiritual rebirth means and how it manifests itself in the life of one who is truly born again.

The Bible addresses this very concern. Paul writes, "What shall we say then? Are we to continue in sin so that grace may increase? May it never be! How shall we who died to sin still live in it? Therefore, we have been buried with Him through baptism into death, so that as Christ was raised from the dead through the glory of the Father, so we too might walk in newness of life" (Ro 6:1–2, 4).

John MacArthur adds this point of clarification: "Grace does not grant permission to live in the flesh; it supplies power to live in the Spirit" (*The Salvation of Babies Who Die-Part I*).

But how do we walk in newness of life? How do we live in the Spirit? Didn't Paul say we are both spirit and flesh, and these two are constantly battling each other within us? Yes, he did. The key to victory, then, is in the work God does within our hearts at the moment we are spiritually reborn.

The Old Testament provides a beautiful illustration of this very work: "Moreover, I will give you a new heart and put a new spirit within you; and I will remove your heart of stone from your flesh. I will put my Spirit within you and cause you to walk in my statutes" (Ez 36:26–27). This is nothing short of a total heart transplant! And notice that last part—God, by giving us a whole new heart, *causes* us to walk in His statutes. This is often lost on the legalist. The beauty of the New Covenant is that God has made the *oughts* of His Word the *wants* of our regenerate heart! This is true freedom. Once we are born again of God's Spirit, we are free to obey Him! No longer do we have to be held in bondage to sin.

Paul wrote, "Having been set free from sin, you became slaves of righteousness" (Ro 6:18 NRSV). Slaves of righteousness? Yes, to the degree that we yield to our rightful master, Jesus Christ. One of the great paradoxes of the gospel is that true freedom means being enslaved to the right master. We can either be enslaved to God and His authority or to sin and its bondage. Our only real freedom is the freedom to choose our master. Dwight Edwards puts it this way:

TRUE FREEDOM MEANS BEING ENSLAVED TO THE RIGHT MASTER.

> True freedom comes only by yielding to His authority, His presence, and His power. As we radically abandon ourselves to our rightful Master, we'll find ourselves in glad bondage, and our souls will sing for joy at coming home. We'll find that the tension is gone between the standard of God's demands and our inner reluctance and inability to meet them. That which was imposed upon us externally is now implanted within us supernaturally through His New Covenant provision of our new disposition and power.
>
> —*RW*, p. 161

This explains how it is that God, in a millisecond, transformed my heart and took away my love for money and all that money represented to me. He removed it from me completely, permanently, and in the blink of an eye. Prior to that transformation, I constantly felt that inner "tension" or struggle Edwards refers to. This was my ongoing inner dialogue: *I know I should be paying my tithe, but boy oh boy, what I could do with that money if I could just invest it in such and such. I'll be generous with my money once I'm really wealthy.* Or, *I know it's important to read my Bible every day and set aside time for prayer, but I literally don't have the time. Between work and studying the stock market, I barely have time to go to the gym!*

Here's what I know for a fact. Before I was born again of God's Spirit, I was a slave to sin. I only felt fulfilled, alive, and excited when I was sinning. I could not conceive of a fun, happy life, for example, without living a worldly, sinful lifestyle. *Live for God? What does that even mean?*

Now, after having been born again, I am a slave to righteous living. By that I mean that I only feel fulfilled, alive, and excited when I am obeying God. When sin creeps back into my life (and it's always trying), it's a total buzz kill. Now, I cannot conceive of a happy, fulfilling life outside of being in God's perfect will for my life. *Live for myself?* Never again—not as long as I am abiding in the true Vine.

I remember a time when I considered this sort of transformation (God doing all the work while I remain the passive recipient) a form of cheating. The religionist might say, "Well, if God does all the work, how will you ever learn how to overcome your weaknesses? How will you ever grow and progress and become more like Christ?" When I was LDS, I very much felt this way; God gave me this brain and these hands, and by golly, I'm going to overcome my sinfulness and shortcomings through sheer grit, self-denial, and willpower.

Let me share with you a perfect example of how God has changed my perspective on spiritual transformation. Sometime in December 2004, as I was making my way through the New Testament in earnest, I came to Titus 2:11–12. In my NIV Bible it reads, "For the grace of God that brings salvation has appeared to all men. It teaches us to say 'No' to ungodliness and worldly passions, and to live self-controlled, upright, and godly lives in this present age."

In my Bible, the lower half of the page opposite this passage is blank, and so I wrote a note to myself regarding these verses. This is what I wrote, verbatim: "Titus 2:11–12 suggests that 'God's grace' teaches us or enables us to say no to worldly temptations—sex, money, power, etc. In other words, it is not merely our will power that will allow us to resist these temptations. It may not even be *primarily* our willpower. This has certainly been my experience."

I am so glad I wrote that thought down; it makes me laugh every time I read it. More than anything, it shows me how far I've come in learning to trust in God's power and not my own, especially in the area of overcoming sin in my life. Notice how I use the word *suggest* in the opening sentence. I was not yet convinced that the Bible was a trustworthy source of absolute truth; although I arrived at that conviction in very short order. Also, notice how I insist on inserting my own willpower into the equation, when, in reality, this passage makes no mention of my willpower at all. Apparently, I was only willing to grant God partial credit for any spiritual transformation in my life. I still needed to make room for my willpower in the process, even if it wasn't the *primary* motivating force.

Six years later, on September 30, 2010, *after* my born-again experience, here is what I wrote just below that first note: "9-30-10 A quick addendum is in order: It is not *at all* our willpower that enables us to resist temptation! Not at all. 'It is the grace of God.' Period. It is the Holy Spirit living in me (by God's grace) that teaches me, allows me, encourages me to rise to that challenge. JBW"

See the difference? By 2010, I had learned to read the Bible and believe in its promises exactly as they are written. Notice how I am not seeking to interpret the passage or insert my own opinion (or ego) into the subject. But more importantly, do you see how I had learned to just trust in God's redeeming power and not in my own inadequate efforts? Remember, this was Paul's frustration with the Galatians: "Are you so foolish? After beginning with the Spirit, are you now trying to attain your goal by human effort?" (Gal 3:3 NIV).

Radical Dependence

Imagine that you win a three-day golf weekend that includes one-on-one golf lessons from Tiger Woods. Over the course of the weekend, he shows you all the finer points of driving, chipping, and putting. He helps you with your swing plane, posture, and rhythm. He even helps you in your decision making—which club to use for different situations on the course. The question is, after extensive instruction from Tiger, would you be able to play just like he does? Of course not. He might improve your game considerably, but it is doubtful that you'd be joining the PGA Tour anytime soon.

Now imagine that in some mysterious way, Tiger Woods was able to assimilate himself into your body so that all of his movements were carried out in your body. He would be able to drive, chip, and putt through you. In other words, it wouldn't really be you golfing but Tiger Woods golfing through you. Sound familiar? It should. Paul wrote, "I have been crucified with Christ; and it is no longer I who live, but Christ lives in me" (Gal 2:20).

This, then, as radical as it may sound to someone accustomed to solving his own problems, overcoming his own sin issues, and proving to God his own worthiness, is the key to true Christian living. We can (and must) get to that point where we acknowledge there is literally nothing we can do in and of ourselves to impress God, serve God, or even obey God. In fact, living the Christian life by our own strength and ability is absolutely impossible. We simply cannot do it. The Christian life is nothing more and nothing less than Christ living in us and through us. The Christian life isn't just trusting in God; it's trusting in God *only*!

THE CHRISTIAN LIFE ISN'T JUST TRUSTING IN GOD; IT'S TRUSTING IN GOD *ONLY!*

Now at this point, I can imagine my LDS reader protesting, "First, you tell me there's nothing I can do to even participate in my own salvation (except receive it as a gift through faith), and now you're telling me I can't even be a true Christian through my own decision making? You're killing me here!" To which I would say, "Yes, that is exactly right."And on this last point, remember that Jesus is telling you that you must die to self. We must die in order to truly live.

Some might counter with Philippians 2:2, which says, in part, "Work out your salvation with fear and trembling …"

See? You have to work at this! God isn't just going to do it for you.

First of all, Paul tells us to work *out* our salvation, not work *at* our salvation. The Greek verb for *work out* means "to continually work to bring something to fulfillment or completion." And while it is certainly the responsibility (and privilege) of every true follower of Jesus to pursue a life of obedience that will bring glory to God, the key to how this comes about is found in the very next verse: "For it is *God who is at work in you*, both to will and to work for His good pleasure" (Phil 2:13, italics mine).

So, even when you *think* you're doing pretty well—attending all your church meetings, resisting drugs and alcohol, and helping the needy—it is actually "God who is at work in you." What a blow to the ego, right? Right. Death to self.

If we are ever going to call out to God in desperate dependence, we must embrace our inadequacies. We have got to see our own brokenness and accept ourselves for who we really are, in the flesh at least. Remember, it was Paul who had the courage to proclaim: "For I know that nothing good dwells in me, that is, in my flesh; for the willing is present in me, but the doing of the good is not" (Ro 7:18).

This was perhaps the hardest thing for me to accept as I emerged out of the "God's grace, plus my efforts" of Mormonism and into the "Christ and Christ alone" of biblical Christianity.

You mean to tell me that *nothing* good dwells in me?

Well, if nothing good dwelt in Paul (the greatest missionary who ever lived), I guarantee you that nothing good dwells in us.

The flesh (ego) resists this with all its might. "How dare you cut me out of the equation!" it says. But remember, we are called to live up to God's standard of righteousness, for the purpose of bringing Him glory, solely by His Spirit. We have to consistently do the right things, for the right reasons, by the right power. These are God's standards.

Still think you can do it? I'll save you the suspense. You cannot. And as it turns out, it was never intended that you would be able to. Christ Himself set this precedent.

We learned in Philippians 2 that Christ "... although He existed in the form of God ... emptied Himself, taking the form of a bond-servant, being made in the likeness of men" (vv. 5–7). So we see that, temporarily, Jesus divested Himself of His heavenly glory and chose to humble himself, appearing as a mere man. But it's what we learn about Him in the gospel of John that is truly amazing. Jesus stated very simply in John 5:30, "By myself I can do nothing." Earlier in the chapter, He provided some clarification of how this could be: "Truly, truly, I say to you, the Son can do nothing of Himself, unless it is something He sees the Father doing; for whatever the Father does, these things the Son also does in like manner" (Jn 5:19).

Jesus was adamant that His disciples understand this key principle. He didn't want to give them golf lessons; He wanted to golf in them and through them by the power of His Spirit. Before He was tried and crucified, Jesus said this to His disciples: "But I tell you the truth, it is to your advantage that I go away; for if I do not go away, the Helper will not come to you; but if I go, I will send Him to you" (Jn 16:7).

The last lesson Jesus ever taught His disciples was an expansion of this very principle.

The Vine and the Branches

In the Gospel of John, Jesus made seven powerful declarations about Himself; we call these the seven "I Am" statements of Christ. Jesus said: "I Am the Bread of Life." "I Am the Light of the World." "I Am the Gate." "I Am the

Good Shepherd." "I Am the Resurrection and the Life." "I Am the Way, the Truth, and the Life." "I Am the Vine."

Jesus may very well have saved His best for last when He laid out His final object lesson to His beloved disciples. He knew that even if His disciples hadn't caught on quite yet, His time with them on this earth had drawn to a close. What He desired for them above all else at that moment was that they understand their role going forward. So He unveiled yet another powerful paradox of the gospel. Let's read John 15:1–5:

> I am the true vine, and my Father is the vinedresser. Every branch in Me that does not bear fruit, He takes away; and every branch that bears fruit, He prunes it so that it may bear more fruit. You are already clean because of the word which I have spoken to you. Abide in Me, and I in you. As the branch cannot bear fruit of itself unless it abides in the vine, so neither can you unless you abide in Me. I am the vine, you are the branches; he who abides in Me and I in him, he bears much fruit, for apart from Me you can do nothing.

If you've ever walked through a vineyard, you know that the vine is essentially the trunk of the grape plant. It's thick and somewhat gnarly as it emerges out of the earth and grows up to about six feet tall. The branches, on the other hand, are delicate and thin. The vinedresser carefully props up the branches, keeping them up and off the ground by arranging them horizontally along trellises. This keeps the branches clean from dirt and debris and also optimizes the amount of sunlight the branches receive. But the trellises perform another, even more critical function; they help to keep the branches securely connected to the vine. This, then, is the image to which Jesus wants to draw their attention.

"I am the vine, you are the branches." Clearly, Jesus is teaching them that just as a branch can never produce fruit if it is disconnected from the vine, neither will they ever be able to "bear fruit" if they are separated from Him. Because the life-giving nourishment is drawn up out of the earth and through the vine, the branches must remain firmly connected to the vine if they are to have any hope of actually yielding grapes! In the same way, Christ is the sole source of our spiritual nourishment. Remember, He is both the Bread of Life and the source of Living Water. Ultimately, He *is* the Life and there is no other source of life.

It is far beyond the scope of this book to go into great detail regarding the three groups of people to which Jesus is referring—those that bear no fruit, those that bear some fruit, and those that bear much fruit. For a wonderful, detailed discussion of John 15, I recommend Bruce Wilkinson's book *Secrets of the Vine*. For our purposes, let's focus on those that bear much fruit: those that *abide* in the vine.

Abide … that is such a passive verb. It's hard to get excited about an activity as passive as abiding. Typically, we get fired up when called to action, not passivity. And yet here we have Jesus gathering His little team of fishermen and tanners and other such nobodies with this battle cry: "Okay, men, once I'm gone, I want you to get out there and … abide." Jesus, of course, as "author and perfecter of our faith," knows the tremendous power behind these words that are inherent within this simple commitment to abide in Him.

Have you ever walked past an apricot tree and heard its little branches and buds groaning and straining to squeeze out fruit? Of course not. It just happens naturally as each of the parts of the tree performs its God-given role. Sugars and moisture flow easily up through the roots, into the trunk, up to the branches, and ultimately, to the buds that receive these nutrients in order to become apricots. By the same token, the most fruitful, abundant life we could possibly live is predicated on our ability to simply remain connected to our spiritual life source, Jesus Christ.

This runs counter to religions that emphasize doing, striving, proving, and qualifying. And while the LDS church certainly does advocate spending quality time reading the scriptures and praying, I believe there is far too much emphasis on doing—doing your home teaching, going to the temple, magnifying your calling, paying your tithing, etc. It's no wonder that one of the most beloved LDS hymns says, "Put your shoulder to the wheel, push along. Do your duty with a heart full of song" ("Put Your Shoulder to the Wheel," *LDS Hymnal*).

Now, please don't get me wrong. Doing good works and being obedient to God's commandments are extremely important to the Christian life. The difference is the mature Christian understands that his good works and obedience are merely by-products of his close, intimate, relationship with the Lord. The mature Christian simply abides in the vine; his shoulder is automatically set to the wheel. But it's not really a push. God's Spirit *pulls* us into acts of service and righteous living. In fact, this is precisely what Jesus means when He says, "He who abides in Me and I in him, he bears much fruit."

Bearing Fruit

What does it mean then to bear fruit? In simplest terms, it means that we live lives that glorify God and draw others to Him. It means that we submit daily to His perfect will for our lives, which, without fail, will include obedience to His commandments and acts of love and service to our fellow man. It means that we are being transformed, over time, into the image of Christ. Paul put it this way: "… present your bodies a living and holy sacrifice, acceptable to God, which is your acceptable service of worship. And do not be conformed to this world, but be transformed by the renewing of your mind, so that you may prove what the will of God is, that which is good and acceptable and perfect" (Ro 12:1–2).

And to the saints in Corinth, Paul writes, "But we all, with unveiled face, beholding as in a mirror the glory of the Lord, are being transformed into the same image from glory to glory, just as from the Lord, the Spirit" (2 Cor 3:18).

This process of transformation, which begins with a rebellious, unregenerate heart and ends with the image (and characteristics) of Christ overlaid onto us, is what we call *sanctification*. We are justified (made right with God) at the moment we place our faith and trust in Christ. We are sanctified gradually, over the course of our entire lives, as we submit to the cleansing power of God's Spirit. And allowing God to sanctify us is the primary way in which we bear fruit.

But clearly bearing fruit also includes obedience to God and caring for the needs of others (i.e., good works). James makes this crystal clear: "Pure and undefiled religion in the sight of our God and Father is this: to visit the orphans and widows in their distress, and to keep oneself unstained by the world" (Jas 1:27). This is religion; in other words, it's Christian living. It is not salvation. As true followers of Jesus, we have the opportunity and privilege to do good works. These good works don't save us, but they do provide outward evidence of our inner, saving faith. Remember, we are saved by faith alone, but saving faith is never alone; it is always accompanied by good works.

CHAPTER 19

A PLACE FOR WORKS

> But prove yourselves doers of the word, and not merely hearers who delude themselves.
>
> —James 1:22

I met with a young man recently who clearly had lost his testimony of Joseph Smith, the Book of Mormon, and the LDS church as God's one true church. And although he had already made up his mind to leave the church, he didn't know what he was leaving it for. The thought of not belonging to a church terrified him and gave him an intense feeling of insecurity.

He confided in me that the one thing that bothered him most was leaving a highly structured church environment with "many opportunities to serve" and going into what he called "total nothingness." His perception was that born-again Christians, by putting so much emphasis on salvation by God's grace, are rarely if ever motivated to do good works.

He asked me, for example, what my "calling" was in my church, Calvary Chapel Westgrove. Well, of course, I don't exactly have a calling in the sense he referred to, but I did share with him all the things I do voluntarily in and through Westgrove. I told him that I serve as an usher on Sunday mornings and lecture on Tuesday evenings (what we call TNT, Tuesday Night Training) on a variety of subjects, ranging from inter-religious studies to molecular biology as proof of intelligent design. And I commented that I love going on relief missions to third-world countries (mainly as a dentist).

Interestingly, even though I told him that I spend far more time serving in my current church than I ever did as a Latter-day Saint, he still wasn't satisfied. It just wasn't structured enough for him. Because what I do isn't technically a calling given to me by some church authority above me, it was just too flimsy for his tastes. At any moment, according to him, I could just walk away from all of these acts of service and still be in perfectly good standing with God. I assured him that I could indeed. But why on earth, I asked him, would I deny myself such wonderful opportunities to serve, from which I derive so much joy?

He seemed baffled, and all he could say was, "But you could, though [walk away]."

Let's go back, just one more time, I promise, to one of the foundational passages of this book, Ephesians 2:8–10. But this time, we're going to take a closer look at verse 10 (italics mine): "For by grace you have been saved through faith; and that not of yourselves, it is the gift of God; not as a result of works, so that no one may boast. For we are His workmanship, *created in Christ Jesus for good works*, which God prepared beforehand so that we would walk in them."

Yes, we are saved by grace,through faith. But what are we saved *for*? Good works! God had no intention of saving us so that we could just sit around and marinate in our own salvation. He wants us to live abundantly, abiding in His Word, drinking deeply from the well of living water, serving others, and in so doing, bringing glory to Him! He wants the unbeliever to see our lives and ask us, "What do you have that I don't have?"

Peter writes, "Keep your behavior excellent among the Gentiles, so that in the thing in which they slander you as evildoers, they may because of your good deeds, as they observe them, glorify God in the day of visitation" (1 Pt 2:12). This is how we do our part in saving souls. This is how we bear much fruit. And so to this soon-to-be ex-Mormon young man, all I could really say was that if his perception is that born-again Christians somehow lack the motivation or opportunities to serve the Lord and perform good works, he probably just hasn't met the right kind of born-again Christians.

And to my LDS reader, if this is also your perception (and chances are, it is), let me assure you that the mature Christian who has been born again of God's Spirit and is abiding in the Vine of Christ understands very well his call to good works. The New Testament continually reminds the true follower of

Jesus that he is saved by grace in order to do good works. Here are just two of the many passages that compliment Ephesians 2:

> And God is able to make all grace abound to you, so that always having all sufficiency in everything, you may have an abundance for every good deed.
>
> —2 Corinthians 9:8

> He saved us, not on the basis of deeds which we have done in righteousness, but according to His mercy … so that those who have believed God will be careful to engage in good deeds.
>
> —Titus 3:5, 8

Does this make sense now? We are not saved by our obedience to God or our good works. Our obedience is never good enough, and insisting that our good works somehow contribute to our salvation is essentially saying that Christ's sacrifice was not a finished work! Rather, we are saved by grace, through faith in Christ. Our obedience and good works flow from our salvation. We fight *from* victory, not *for* victory. And the difference between the two, I can tell you from first-hand experience, is night and day.

To illustrate how Christ's finished work of salvation translates into a life of good works on our part, let me share with you an allegory.

Good Fortune at the Grocery Store

A woman who is struggling to make ends meet is standing in the checkout line at the grocery store. She wonders if the $75.00 in her purse will even cover the measly items in her cart. Luckily, the macaroni and cheese is on sale, ten for $10.00!

As it turns out, the shopper in front of her in line is an exceedingly wealthy and generous woman. For the purposes of our story, we'll say that her resources are unlimited. The wealthy woman, perceiving the financial distress of the woman behind her, discretely arranges with the cashier to cover the full cost of her groceries. She doesn't do this out of pity or because she perceives that the poor woman *deserves* it, per se. For all she knows,the woman behind her in line might be a really rotten person. She does it purely out of compassion. She perceives a need and is able and willing to fill that need.

When it's finally the poor woman's turn to check out, the cashier politely informs her that her total of $73.67 has been paid in full by the previous customer, who, by this time, is long gone (as she had designed).

The poor woman's jaw drops. Tears begin to well up in her eyes as she processes this amazing display of kindness from a complete stranger. Nothing like this has ever happened to her before. She is speechless.

The poor woman digs into her purse, grabs a $20 bill, and extends it to the cashier. "Surely I can pay *something* toward my groceries."

"Uh, actually, no. There's a zero balance. The way our system works, you can't pay anything even if you want to," the cashier replies. "Your groceries were paid in full."

At this point, the poor woman is just bursting with gratitude toward her generous benefactor, but she's long gone! Certainly there is *something* she can do for *someone*.

Instinctively, she knows what to do. She hands the $20 bill to the cashier and with a smile says, "Please take this. Maybe now you need this more than I."

Now it is the cashier who is speechless, tears welling up in *her* eyes, as she gratefully accepts the much-needed money.

And so it is when God's grace captures our hearts. It's an "I just want to jump out of my skin" sort of love and compassion that we feel toward others. I can't really pay God back anything. After all, the entire universe already belongs to Him. But I can bless others. I can reflect His love in a way that others would want to know Him and receive eternal life too. My love and gratitude sort of squirts out the sides, as it were, horizontally toward others. And I can do this consistently "unto the least of these."

Rewards in Heaven

Before we leave this discussion on good works, I need to clarify an important point of biblical doctrine that many Latter-day Saints are unaware of. And I hope this helps my LDS reader more fully appreciate the biblical view of the glory of heaven and the fairness of our just God.

You will remember that in the parable of the laborers, Jesus clearly taught that regardless of whether you worked twelve hours in the field or just one hour, the reward was to be the same: one denarius. He was referring to salvation, our entrance into heaven, and we know this because Jesus begins the parable by saying, "For the kingdom of heaven is like a landowner …" (Mt 20:1).

Now, can you imagine how this teaching might have been received by the law-abiding, righteous Jews of that era? These were the twelve-hour laborers, and I can only assume that they would have been repulsed by Jesus' radical, new teaching that, because of God's graciousness, even lowly, far less qualified people would go to the exact same heaven as they. Most Mormons I know, however, don't really have to use their imagination on this one, because many bristle at this in much the same way. I know I sure did. How could this possibly be fair?

Here's what the Bible teaches. Salvation, eternal life in God's glorious kingdom, is a free gift to all who come to saving faith in Christ. This amazing gift is equally distributed (one denarius) because it is predicated solely on the imputed righteousness of Christ, which is perfect and unchanging. There is one gift and one giver. All receive equally. This is our entrance into heaven.

But once we are in heaven, there are different rewards given to the faithful, in varying "degrees of glory." Now, I am not referring to the degrees of glory as found in D&C 76. These are unique to Joseph Smith and Mormon theology. But if it helps you better understand the fairness of heaven, you can sort of think of it like that.

In his second letter to the Corinthians, Paul is ruminating on how wonderful heaven is going to be and how he really would prefer to be "absent from the body and to be at home with the Lord" (2 Cor 5:8.). And then he makes this very important point: "Therefore we also have as our ambition, whether at home or absent, to be pleasing to Him. For we must all appear before the *judgment seat of Christ*, so that each one may be recompensed for his deeds in the body, according to what he has done, whether good or bad" (2 Cor 5:9–10, italics mine).

Three things need to be clarified from this passage. First, this is not a general epistle written to anyone and everyone. Paul is specifically writing to the saints in Corinth; these were people who had come to saving faith in Christ already. (This will be important to remember when we get to the third point, regarding this judgment seat of Christ.)

Second, Paul makes clear reference to rewards (recompense) in heaven based on our deeds while we're here on this earth. In fact, he's not too shy to admit that our prime ambition can and should be to "be pleasing to Him" in order to receive these rewards. And what exactly are these rewards in heaven? Well, we really don't know; the Bible doesn't exactly spell it out very clearly. But Paul does give us a hint in a passage very familiar to the Latter-day Saint; although, I am hoping that now you can see it in a new light. Paul writes, "There are also heavenly bodies and earthly bodies, but the glory of the heavenly is one, and the glory of the earthly is another. There is one glory of the sun, and another glory of the moon, and another glory of the stars, for star differs from star in glory. So also is the resurrection of the dead" (1 Cor 15:40–42).

So, what does this all mean? Again, we just don't know—not exactly anyway. But we're not left totally in the dark. Paul's allusion to the relative glory of the sun, moon, and stars and how it relates to the resurrection of the dead might mean this: the amazingly faithful saints of the past and present, such as Job, Esther, Daniel, John, etc., will shine very brightly, like the sun, in God's kingdom. Other faithful believers who did not contribute quite as much to God's kingdom while here on this earth, but who still bore fruit, might shine like the moon. Still others, who may have just squeaked into heaven by the seat of their pants (the one-hour laborers), but who did come to saving faith in Christ, will likely shine like the stars. But shine they will, because God's kingdom is just that glorious. Everything shines.

GOD'S KINGDOM IS JUST THAT GLORIOUS. EVERYTHING SHINES.

Third, what is the "judgment seat of Christ," and how does it differ from the "great white throne" judgment found in Revelation 20?

The great white throne is where all those not found in the "book of life" are judged for their evil deeds and refusal to accept God's gift of eternal life through His Son. These are those destined for eternal darkness. Revelation 20:13 says, "And the sea gave up the dead which were in it, and death and Hades gave up the dead which were in them; and they were judged, every one of them, for their deeds."

The judgment seat of Christ is an entirely different platform, however—literally. This term "judgment seat" is a direct translation of the Greek word, *bema*, which refers to the elevated platform where victorious athletes (e.g., during the Olympics) stood to receive their crowns. Today, of course, we award the gold, silver, and bronze medals to Olympic athletes, and at the awards ceremony they stand side by side, but at slightly different elevations. All three are winners, and yet we recognize their performances relative to each other with gold, silver, and bronze. That's kind of like the sun, moon, and stars. Likewise, the victorious believer is "judged" at the bema seat of Christ in order to receive his or her rewards in heaven.

CHAPTER 20

SIN AND FORGIVENESS (A FAMILY MATTER)

> God deals with you as with sons; for what son is there whom his father does not discipline?
>
> —Hebrews 12:7

My LDS uncle posed an interesting question to me in the form of a hypothetical situation. He wanted to know what I thought about the Christian pastor, a man well known for his hard work and good deeds (for some reason my uncle needed to add to the story that this pastor really was a "good person"), who, in the heat of passion, commits adultery with his secretary. It's a one-time occurrence, and he feels really bad about it. However, for fear of losing his marriage and his church, he decides to keep it a secret. He prays to God and asks His forgiveness and feels that that's enough.

I'll tell you what my response was shortly, but for now I want to focus on the larger context of our discussion that night. Many Latter-day Saints, my uncle included, feel that the Christian's view of sin and repentance is too flimsy. Sin is too easily tolerated, and the repentance "process" lacks real teeth. When viewed from the Mormon perspective, I can easily understand their concerns.

The LDS church teaches that true repentance is a six-step process, and each step is critical to the sinner's receiving forgiveness. These are: 1) Recognize that you have sinned. 2) Feel sorrow for the sin. 3) Confess the sin to God and bishop. 4) Ask forgiveness of God and others. 5) Make restitution for the sin. 6) Forsake the sin forever and ever. Because of the implicit finality in the last step, any return to a particular sin would render the entire six-step process null and void.

President Spencer W. Kimball, apparently feeling that the above process *still* wasn't enough, raised the repentance bar even higher, adding the elements of works and uncertainty to the equation. Kimball wrote:

> Your Heavenly Father has promised forgiveness upon total repentance and meeting all requirements, but that forgiveness is not granted merely for the asking. There must be works—many works—and an all-out, total surrender, with a great humility and a "broken heart and contrite spirit." It depends upon you whether or not you are forgiven, and when. It could be weeks, it could be years, it could be centuries before that happy day when you have the positive assurance that the Lord has forgiven you. That depends upon your humility, your sincerity, your works, your attitudes.
>
> —*Miracle of Forgiveness*, pp. 324–5

Apparently, according to President Kimball, the responsibility and weight of forgiveness rest primarily upon the penitent sinner. "It depends upon *you* whether or not you are forgiven." I forced myself to reread *Miracle of Forgiveness* last year, albeit from the perspective of being twenty years removed from Mormonism. I came away with the thought that this book did indeed have an appropriate title. According to President Kimball, it literally takes a *miracle* to ever receive God's forgiveness. This might be Mormon legalism at its finest.

In fact, this system of repentance, lifted directly from the Old Testament, was perfectly suitable for Israel under the Law of Moses. It was suitable because Israel had not yet been redeemed; Jesus had not yet come to pay the penalty for sin. Remember, Paul wrote to the Galatians that the law was put in place as a "schoolmaster" to convince the children of Israel of their sinfulness. It was never meant to produce personal righteousness sufficient for salvation. On the contrary, their form of repentance was really more punitive than salvific.

And so with that in mind, let's look at a quote from President Kimball at General Conference, May, 1975: "There can be no forgiveness without real and total repentance, and there can be no repentance without punishment. This is as eternal as the soul."

Technically, President Kimball is right; there can be no forgiveness without punishment. This, of course, is precisely why Jesus came to suffer and die on the cross—to bear the punishment for our sins! He was punished so that we wouldn't have to be. Unfortunately, this is not what Kimball is referring to. It amazes me how consistently President Kimball's teachings are in direct conflict with those of the Bible.

To further illustrate my point, the apostle John wrote:

> We have come to know and have believed the love which God has for us. God is love, and the one who abides in love abides in God, and God abides in him. By this, love is perfected with us, so that we may have confidence in the day of judgment … *There is no fear in love*; but perfect love casts out fear; *because fear involves punishment, and the one who fears is not perfected in love.*
>
> —1 John 4:16–18, italics mine

I am left to wonder how a church that professes to be Christian could so consistently miss the meaning and purpose of the cross of Jesus. One would think, based on their doctrines of sin, repentance, and salvation that the Latter-day Saints jump directly from Malachi over to 1 Nephi. The New Testament and the gospel of grace so beautifully explained therein simply do not figure into Mormon teachings.

So, what does the New Testament have to say about repentance and forgiveness? John, in his first epistle, describes the new dynamic available to all those who have been adopted into the family of God, those who have been born again of God's Spirit, those who now "walk in the Light." In 1 John 1:7 we read: "But if we walk in the Light as He Himself is in the Light, we have fellowship with one another, and the blood of Jesus His Son cleanses us from all sin."

What does this tell us? It tells us that, for those who are truly sons and daughters of God, sin is dealt with as a family matter. As we walk in the light of God's love, we are continually sheltered by God's mercy and grace. We are, on an ongoing basis, cleansed from our sins by the blood of Jesus.

To illustrate this point, imagine that a stranger breaks into your home in the middle of the night wielding a baseball bat. He goes into your living room with that bat and demolishes two lamps, several fine porcelain dolls, and a very expensive mirror! What would you do, assuming you could somehow detain him? You'd call 911 and have the police arrest him, of course. And chances are, you'd have him prosecuted to the full extent of the law.

Now, suppose your seventeen-year-old son is horsing around one night with his buddies in that same living room, playing with an old piñata they found in the garage and, you guessed it, a baseball bat. Suppose that in a moment of carelessness, your son busts up two lamps, several fine porcelain dolls, and a very expensive mirror. What do you do? Call 911? Have him arrested? Of course not. But why not? The same exact damage was incurred in both scenarios. The fact is that you're going to deal with your son differently because, well, he's your son. He belongs to you. You love him. He's going to need to mow lawns to pay for the damage but at no point do you kick him out of the house or disown him as your child. In the same way, we do not lose our salvation when we sin, any more than we gain our salvation by not sinning.

WE DO NOT LOSE OUR SALVATION WHEN WE SIN, ANY MORE THAN WE GAIN OUR SALVATION BY NOT SINNING.

And so what exactly is the process by which a son or daughter of God receives forgiveness for sin? According to the Bible, it is a one-step process. John explains, "If we confess our sins, He is faithful and righteous to forgive us our sins and to cleanse us from all unrighteousness" (1 Jn 1:9). According to the Bible, then, our sole responsibility is to confess our sins. God does the rest. He is faithful and righteous to forgive us our sins.

This, then, was my response to my uncle regarding his hypothetical story of the philandering pastor. In his scenario, the pastor had sinned against his wife and his flock and, therefore, would need to confess to them as well. That's difficult to do but necessary; otherwise, he would simply be converting one sin (adultery) into another sin—ongoing deceit. This was King David's strategy until he was confronted by Nathan the prophet with his egregious sins. David was slowly dying inside until he was honest in acknowledging his awful deeds. And when he did, God was faithful to forgive him and restore to him every blessing imaginable. That is not to say David didn't pay a steep price for the sins he committed. But even in those hardships, God was gracious to him.

As a side note: King David might not have been the best example to use in this case because of the fact that Joseph Smith taught that there was not, and never will be, forgiveness for David due to his role in the death of Uriah the Hittite. David, according to Mormon teaching, was cast into outer darkness forever. This, for me anyway, prompts two questions. First, what are we to make of the majority of the book of Psalms, which reflects David's tribute and praise to his gracious, forgiving God? And second, if David really had never been forgiven, why would Jesus proudly accept the title of Son of David a thousand years later? But I digress.

A Life of Faithfulness

I recently heard a pastor on the radio who taught that living a life of faithfulness is not so much *our* always being faithful to God (which we never fully are) but rather living a life in which we continually acknowledge *His* faithfulness in forgiving us! In fact, this very concept is one of the keys to what motivates us to repent of our sins to begin with. We read in Paul's letter to the Romans: "Or do you think lightly of the riches of His kindness and tolerance and patience, not knowing that *the kindness of God leads you to repentance*?" (Ro 2:4, italics mine). Imagine that; the kindness of God leads us to repentance. But this only makes perfect sense.

IMAGINE THAT; THE KINDNESS OF GOD LEADS US TO REPENTANCE.

Remember our imaginary story of Uncle Fred and how he bought a beautiful home for his nephew and his wife? Remember how we decided that the kids would likely go out of their way to take good care of their aging uncle? It would be hard to imagine them ever harming their uncle in any way, but if they were to, it would seem likely that they would swiftly make amends. And so it is with the abiding Christian.

My pastor once compared the sins of the worldly and the sins of the true Christian to a pig and a sheep that fall into the mud. The pig falls into the mud and feels very comfortable there. In fact, he prefers it in the mud and has no real intention of getting out. The sheep, on the other hand, falls into the mud and immediately desires to get out of it. He hates being covered in mud and desperately wants to be washed clean of it. However, let's not lose sight of the fact that both animals fall into the mud from time to time. Christians are nothing more than sinners saved by grace. We are never sinless, but we should sin less and less as we are sanctified over time.

John acknowledges this very thing in the next chapter: "My little children, I am writing these things to you so that you may not sin. And if anyone sins, we have an Advocate with the Father, Jesus Christ the righteous; and He is the propitiation for our sins" (1 Jn 2:1–2). In other words, stay out of the mud, please. But if you do fall in, turn to Jesus, who will not only pull you out of the mud but also will wash you clean. "Though your sins are red like crimson, they will be like wool" (Is 1:18).

And finally, let's address one last issue regarding sin that often comes up in the Mormon-Christian debate. Latter-day Saints seem deeply concerned for the Christian who professes faith in Christ and claims to be saved by grace and yet carries on a life of overt sinfulness. I would first reiterate that any true follower of Christ would have the very same concern for this individual. And we would derive this concern from an unequivocally stern passage found in Hebrews 10:26, 29, and 31:

> For if we go on sinning willfully after receiving the knowledge of the truth, there no longer remains a sacrifice for sins, but a terrifying expectation of judgment ... How much severer punishment do you think he will deserve who has trampled under foot the Son of God, and has regarded as unclean the blood of the covenant by which he was sanctified, and has insulted the Spirit of grace? It is a terrifying thing to fall into the hands of the living God.

What a chilling passage, especially to people like me, who, up until just a few years ago, professed saving faith in Christ and yet sinned willfully against God. According to the Bible, I would have faced judgment and fallen into the hands of the living God. That is terrifying indeed.

The irony, as we talked about previously, is that Mormons pretend to be hard on sin while accusing Christians of being too soft. And yet, LDS doctrine teaches that liars, adulterers, thieves, and even those who never come to saving faith in Christ in this life or the next still enter into a degree of glory. Christians believe that those who profess Christ ("Lord, Lord" Mt 7:22) but do not live a life that honors Him will be judged and cast out into darkness ("Depart from me you workers of iniquity. I never knew you." Mt 7:23) So, yes, we are saved by grace, but we never want to "insult the Spirit of grace" (Heb 10:29).

CHAPTER 21

SECURE IN OUR SALVATION

Who will separate us from the love of Christ?

—Romans 8:35

I've held the opinion that Mormons and Christians view each with what I call a *mutual perception of arrogance*. This is unfortunate. Christians view Mormons as arrogant for claiming they belong to the one true church on the face of the earth and they alone possess the authority (priesthood) to act in God's name. Mormons, on the other hand, view Christians as arrogant (or at least presumptuous) for claiming that they *know* they are saved and that when they die, they will live forever in the presence of the Lord in His kingdom. As we discussed in Chapter 7, the Latter-day Saint tends to recoil at this thought and feels that it is, essentially, counting one's chickens before they hatch.

My experience is that neither camp perceives the other correctly. I have met very few truly arrogant Mormons in my forty-seven years (excluding myself!). Most Latter-day Saints are just grateful to belong to what they believe to be the "one true church." But Mormons misunderstand the Christian who says he *knows* he's going to heaven when he dies. It would indeed be an arrogant statement if the Christian believed he was going to heaven based even partly on his obedience and good works. But that is not what the Christian means. What he's saying is this: "I know I'm going to heaven because of what Christ did for me on the cross! God's promise is that if I put all of my faith and trust in Him and Him alone, I will be forgiven my sins and granted entrance into His kingdom. I know that it has nothing at all to do with my works of righteousness because they are nothing but "filthy rags." So, in reality, his certainty of salvation is really the ultimate expression of humility, not arrogance.

But how *can* the Christian say with such confidence that he knows he's going to heaven when he dies? Very simply, the Christian reads the Bible and believes in God's promises found therein. Our loving God wants us to rest in the assurance of our salvation and live our lives with a joyful expectation of all that He promises in the world to come.

Let's look at just a few examples from the New Testament. John writes, "... God has given us eternal life, and this life is in His Son. He who has the Son has the life; he who does not have the Son of God does not have the life. These things I have written to you who believe in the name of the Son of God, *so that you may* know *that you have eternal life*" (1 Jn 5:11–13, italics mine).

Notice, John did not write these things so that we may hope or wish or think that we have eternal life. If we "have the Son," we *know* that we have eternal life! Doesn't this sound a whole lot better than wondering which of the three kingdoms you might end up in, yet not really knowing until you die and face judgment?

IF WE "HAVE THE SON," WE *KNOW* THAT WE HAVE ETERNAL LIFE!

And for those of you who might say that having this assurance of salvation breeds complacency, let me ask you this: who is in a better position to live a fulfilling, generous life that blesses others—the unsuccessful worry-wart or the immensely wealthy man who is set for life? God knows that this assurance of salvation produces an unspeakable joy that emanates from His children and out to those who are searching for this very joy.

The writer of Hebrews contributes this: "For we have become partakers of Christ, if we hold fast the beginning of our assurance firm until the end" (Heb 3:14). This, then, rounds out the fifth and final pillar of our salvation: enduring to the end, holding firm in our assurance that Christ removed all barriers to His Father's kingdom. Notice the writer says we are partakers of Christ *if* we hold to this assurance. This is our fifth responsibility; after we believe, repent, receive, and abide, we endure.

Calvinism, being essentially the opposite of Mormonism as it relates to the assurance of salvation, teaches "once saved, always saved." Most teachers of the Bible today, my pastor included, teach eternal security for the faithful.

Since we are saved by grace through faith in Christ, the only way we could ever lose our salvation would be if we lost our faith in Christ as Savior. Sin won't separate us from God because those sins are already paid for. And occasional doubt won't separate us because we are imperfect beings with limited understanding. So what would separate the faithful from God and His kingdom? Paul answers that question in what might be the most beautiful passage in the entire Bible:

> Who will separate us from the love of Christ? Will tribulation, or distress, or persecution, or famine, or nakedness, or peril, or sword? … But in all these things we are more than conquerors through Him who loved us. For I am convinced that neither death, nor life, nor angels, nor principalities, nor things present, nor things to come, nor powers, nor height, nor depth, nor any other created thing, will be able to separate us from the love of God, which is in Christ Jesus our Lord.
>
> —Romans 8:35, 37–39

This passage absolutely takes my breath away as God's Spirit confirms, somewhere deep in my heart, that Christ's love is bigger than my rebelliousness, bigger than my stupidity, and bigger than any obstacle that could possibly keep me from His eternal presence. Remember, as a true believer in Christ, I belong to the body of Christ. I represent part of what He considers His bride. As such, He loves me and guards me from any and all threats. Nothing, absolutely nothing, separates me from Him once I truly belong to Him.

How do I know this with 100 percent certainty? Jesus Himself has promised it: "My sheep hear My voice, and I know them, and they follow Me; and I give eternal life to them, and they will never perish; and *no one will snatch them out of my hand.* My Father, who has given them to Me, is greater than all; and no one is able to snatch them out of the Father's hand. I and the Father are one" (Jn 10:27–30, italics mine).

Let's just allow Jesus' promise to stand on its own merits. No one steals us away from Him (or His Father) once we truly belong to Him. And who truly belongs to Him? Who is truly saved? I have no idea, but He does. He knows His sheep; we're the ones that hear Him and follow Him. We believe, repent, receive, abide, and endure.

Let the Celebration Begin!

Imagine that you've won the state lottery and your prize, after taxes, is $84 million dollars! And you're not splitting it with anyone; it's yours outright.

They hold a press conference, a televised event, where you're up on a stage, arm in arm with the governor, who is handing you an oversized check for the full amount. There are balloons and a band and just a whole celebration about to erupt.

However, there are two technical requirements that must be fulfilled in order for you to receive that money. Your home state needs to confirm that you are a legal resident of the state and that you have never been convicted of a felony. If you pass these two requirements, the money will be wired into the account of your choosing in thirty days. (And for the sake of our story, let's say that you are indeed a resident of the state and you've never even been convicted of a misdemeanor, let alone a felony.)

My question to you is this: When would you allow yourself to start celebrating? Would you stand stoically up on the stage, holding out until you have confirmation of the wired funds? Would you insist on not counting your chickens before they hatch? Of course not. If you are like most people, you will be jumping around hysterically on that stage, covered in confetti. Why? Because you know you've won fair and square. Furthermore, after this very public celebration with the governor, you know the state's good for the money. You trust in this victory.

This is the best illustration I can give to help my LDS reader understand why it is that the born-again Christian can celebrate his salvation in God's kingdom even though it technically hasn't come to fruition yet. This is why church is an expression of worship and celebration, with music and clapping and tears of joy. For the body of Christ, the assurance of eternal life is like winning the lottery every single day of our lives. How can we not celebrate?

FOR THE BODY OF CHRIST, THE ASSURANCE OF ETERNAL LIFE IS LIKE WINNING THE LOTTERY EVERY SINGLE DAY OF OUR LIVES.

Dwight Edwards wrote this: "Freedom in Christ is a spiritually intoxicating wine, a breath-taking flight into space, a soul-thrilling escape from enemy territory. It's the spiritual exhilaration of having one's soul set free for the high adventure of a God-enabled assault upon life" (*RW*, p. 160).

Does this describe your life? Are you free to fully enjoy your life because you have the absolute assurance of eternal glory? If not, please come place your full faith and trust in Christ's finished work for your salvation. Set aside any religion that teaches you must earn something that was never intended to be earned but rather received. Receive Christ, who is the Way, the Truth, and the Life. Receive Him … and join the celebration.

Conclusion

A friend of mine, who knew I was close to finishing this book, asked me what the three most important points of the book are. If nothing else, I would want my LDS reader to come away with these three things:

1. The Bible *is* the Word of God. It is trustworthy and reliable, able to teach you and guide you through this life and into eternal life.
2. Christ on the cross, suffering and dying to pay the penalty for your sins, *is* the gospel. There is no other gospel, and there is no other name (or combination of names) under heaven by which you can be saved.
3. Any attempt on your part to add to Christ's sacrifice with your own efforts nullifies God's grace and severs you from Christ as Savior. He *is* the Way—and He's not asking for help.

Of the three, I know that this last one is the hardest for the Latter-day Saint to accept. And I should know; it took me nearly nine years to finally lay down my "collaborating efforts" toward my own salvation. Then again, I started with an enormous ego and an entirely unhealthy need to constantly prove myself worthy and capable to God, others, and myself.

To this very point, I want to share with you a wonderful story, an allegory, told by my friend Shawn McCraney in his book *I Was a Born-again Mormon* (pp. 295–299). It's too good to paraphrase and so, with gratitude to Shawn, I will present it exactly as he wrote it.

The Mountain Climber

A group of mountain climbers met at a snowy mountain resort for a pre-climb meeting the night before attempting a rather steep mountain hike beginning at dawn the following day. Climbers of all abilities and countries gathered in the warm, rustic room of the resort to receive instructions from their professional guide.

"I hope," the guide said, holding up a paper high above the two hundred hikers, "that you have all received the list of equipment and supplies you need for our day hike tomorrow."

From the back of the room, a tall, athletic-looking man with a tan face and wild brown hair raised his hand and exclaimed, "I don't mean to be rude, but I think this list is sorely lacking."

The guide smiled broadly and asked the man what he thought was needed.

"Well, for one thing, your list suggests only three items—a twenty-foot rope, a pick-axe, and a bottle of water. From my experience, we're all going to need a lot more equipment than that for this terrain and weather." The rest of the group agreed.

"I've been a guide on this mountain for twenty years," the guide kindly replied, "I know exactly what you'll need, in addition to the clothes on your back, to get to the top of the mountain. And I am very well aware of what will slow you down." He looked at the rest of the group. "You are all welcome to bring along whatever extra equipment you'd like, but all you need is twenty feet of rope, a pick-axe, and a bottle of water."

"Look outside!" the man nearly shouted. "It's snowing! We'll need blankets, tents, extra clothing, maybe even snowshoes!"

A woman from the group stood and earnestly added, "And what if we get stuck up at the top in this storm? What will we eat? How will we cook?"

Smiling, the guide calmly raised his hands, "All you need to bring is twenty feet of rope, a pick-axe, and a bottle of water."

Again, the man at the back of the room disagreed. "Well, I'm following my own instincts and training. Simple logic tells me I need to bring more. In fact, I am so sure that you are wrong on this, I've lost my faith in you as my guide and am going to climb this mountain on my own."

The meeting dismissed, with the rest of the group agreeing to meet at 8:00 a.m. the next morning in the foyer of the lodge.

The following day, the man at the back of the room arrived at the base of the mountain at dawn, fully prepared for every possible emergency or unexpected circumstance. In addition to his twenty feet of rope, pick-axe and bottle of water, he carried some dehydrated food, Sterno, matches, blankets, extra clothing, a sleeping bag, a small oxygen tank, a first-aid kit, extra boots, socks, a collapsible shovel, a tent, utensils, and an extra-large bottle of water. He even packed an inflatable mattress with a C02 charge.

The clouds were gathered at the base of the mountain as he began his ascent; but as he climbed up a sharp incline around the base of the mountain, he broke through the cloud bank and he could see that there were crystal blue skies and sun ahead. He also discovered, however, that the climb was much steeper than he had anticipated. The higher he climbed, the more fatigued he became. His breath became labored, sweat poured from his body, and he was forced to make frequent stops for rest under the weight of his load.

An hour later, the rest of the group gathered and drove to the base of the mountain. Although many of the hikers felt uncertain about the advice of their guide, all had chosen to follow his instructions, and only had brought with them a twenty-foot rope, a pick-axe, and a bottle of water. Flecks of snow ominously gathered on their shoulders as they took the first steps of their hike.

About an hour into the group's climb, after they too had passed through the bad weather along the base trail and moved up under sunny, blue skies, a discarded tent was seen lying at the side of the path. About a quarter of a mile ahead, the group came upon a blanket roll, a small stove, and a pair of snowshoes. Each passing mile presented newly discarded items. Four hours later at the halfway mark, the group found the man from the back of the room, sitting exhausted, and carrying only a twenty-foot rope, a pick-axe, and a bottle of water. All around him were piles of discarded goods and equipment that other hikers had abandoned over the years. As the group stopped to rest and consume the hot lunch the resort helicopter delivered, the guide took the time to speak with the exhausted, lone climber.

"I understand your desire to be prepared," he said. "I also understand your wanting to approach this hike in what you really believed was the right way. But you not only made it far too difficult on yourself, you assumed you knew better than your guide."

The man took a sip form his water bottle and humbly replied, "You were right all along."

The guide gently placed his hand on the contrite man's back and said, "Well, we're halfway there. Are you ready to get to the top?"

Rejuvenated, the man took another swig of water and nodded.

As they walked together toward the waiting group, the guide laughingly asked, "Do you have everything you need?"

Without hesitation the man replied, "I do now."

Come Unto Me

That story moves me very deeply, probably because I was, for most of my life, the arrogant mountain climber who thought he knew better. I believed *in* Christ, but I didn't actually *believe* Him. Surely there had to be more to salvation than just simple faith in His redeeming blood.

There is something else that Jesus said that I never understood or believed. When I was LDS, it often caused me to think that maybe I *was* missing something. Jesus declared, "Come unto Me, all who are weary and heavy-laden, and I will give you rest. Take My yoke upon you and learn from Me, for I am gentle and humble in heart, and you will find rest for your souls. For My yoke is easy and My burden is light" (Mt 11:28–30).

Say what you will about the commandments, requirements, ordinances, duties, obligations, covenants, and expectations inherent within Mormonism, but one thing you cannot say is that the yoke is easy or the burden is light. And I will only speak for myself when I say that I never experienced any "rest for my soul." Quite the contrary; I never felt that I was doing enough. I find it supremely ironic to discover after all these years that, in fact, what I was guilty of was doing *too much*!

In Closing …

In preparing for this book, I finally came to realize why I identify with Paul so much—we have the same heart toward our own people! Although he was called to preach to the Gentiles, Paul never lost his love for or concern over his brothers, the Jews. In Romans 9, he confesses to have "great sorrow and unceasing grief" in his heart because of the stubbornness of Israel. Of course, by this time, Paul was considered a rebel, a heretic, and a hopeless apostate by the very men he had learned under as a youth and worshipped with as a man (boy, can I relate!). Then again, they weren't there with him on the road to Damascus the day Christ came and made all things new for Paul. And so, for him, there was no turning back, but apparently, there was also no convincing the Jews that their law had been fulfilled in Christ. Even so, Paul never lost hope.

Paul wrote (of the Jews):

> Brethren, my heart's desire and my prayer to God for them is for their salvation. For I testify about them that they have a zeal for God, but not in accordance with knowledge. *For not knowing about God's righteousness and seeking to establish their own*, they did not subject themselves to the righteousness of God. For Christ is the end of the law for righteousness to everyone who believes.
>
> —Romans 10:1–4, italics mine

Paul further clarifies the Jews' dilemma with this: "What shall we say then? That Gentiles, who did not pursue righteousness, attained righteousness, even the righteousness which is by faith; but Israel, pursuing a law of righteousness, did not arrive at that law. Why? Because *they did not pursue it by faith, but as though it were by works*. They stumbled over the stumbling stone" (Ro 9:30–32, italics mine).

I'm not nearly as eloquent as Paul, of course, but let me share with you my own modern parallel: I really want nothing more than for Mormons, en masse, to come to place all their faith and trust in Christ and Christ alone.

I can attest to the fact that Mormons are among the hardest-working, most honest, well-intentioned people in the world. They have an amazing zeal for pleasing God, but unfortunately, that zeal is misplaced. It is not based on biblical truth. They believe that if they work hard enough, are obedient enough, and purify their hearts and minds sufficiently, then they will be "worthy to return to live with Heavenly Father." What they are not aware of is the *divine exchange*, Christ's righteousness imputed to them in exchange for their sinfulness—if they will but believe and receive. They think they have to establish their own righteousness, which, as we all discover sooner or later, is never righteous enough.

I know it bothers most Mormons to hear born-again Christians say they know they're going to heaven when they die. But this is only because they (the Christians) have chosen to receive this divine exchange. They know their salvation has nothing at all to do with their ability to be good enough. Their righteousness (right standing with God) comes solely from the grace of God and is by faith—as promised in God's Word. But because of long-standing, thoroughly ingrained doctrines of *Jesus, plus*, best exemplified by the third Article of Faith, the Latter-day Saints have a hard time accepting this. They have stumbled over the stumbling stone. Unfortunately, this stumbling stone is the cross of Jesus. My greatest fear is that my Mormon loved ones are guilty of mocking the "simplicity of the cross."

Some of you may be on the fence even now. You've been LDS most or all of your life, and yet you see now the surpassing beauty of the gospel of grace and how radically different (and better) it is compared to what you've been taught. The message of the cross rings supremely true to you. But maybe you're afraid—afraid of being wrong, afraid of being rejected by family, afraid of being cast into outer darkness. Having these fears is only natural. Working through them is necessary.

Let me make this really simple for you. In the book of Revelation, the glorified, resurrected Jesus said, "Behold, I stand at the door and knock; if anyone hears My voice and opens the door, I will come in to him and will dine with him, and he with Me" (Rv 3:20).

Open the door. He'll do the rest.

APPENDIX A

For those of you who have already left the LDS church, or are seriously considering leaving but really don't know where to turn, I would like to suggest two powerful resources that will help you regain your spiritual footing and trust in our loving Father.

The first is a wonderful DVD and accompanying workbook called *Transitions: the Mormon Migration from Religion to Relationship.* The DVD is broken down into six, half-hour video segments, which cover everything from the emotional impact of leaving the church, to coping with a new and sometimes strained family dynamic, to what it means to have a relationship with Christ apart from religion. *Transitions* is, without question, the most carefully crafted, diplomatic, and sensitive resource you will find to help you in this journey.

For those living in Utah or Idaho, there are dozens of churches that offer *Transitions* classes hosted by former Mormons who have already made this journey ... and lived to tell about it. And if you live in Southern California, feel free to come to my church, Calvary Chapel Westgrove in Garden Grove, where I myself guide transitioners through the six-week course. Perhaps you'd prefer to go through the series yourself in the privacy of your own home. That's okay too. You can order the DVD and workbook or locate a church near you that offers *Transitions* by going to: www.LDStransitions.com.

Second, I highly recommend Carma Naylor's magnificent two-volume book called *A Mormon's Unexpected Journey (Finding the Grace I Never Knew).* It is a powerful and inspiring account of Sister Carma's uncompromising search for truth after having dedicated forty years of faithful service to the LDS church. It is, hands down, the best book ever written on this subject of coming out of Mormonism and into biblical Christianity—and I've read everything! But don't stop at Volume 1, for as good as it is, Volume 2 is even better.

There are many wonderful books, websites, conferences, and support groups that can help you in your transition. But these two resources are the best available and great places to start!

APPENDIX B

Sometime in the summer of 2013, I sent an advance copy of this book to a very close friend of mine, who is as devout a Mormon as you will find. Mike (not his real name) was, for years, a bishop in his hometown and currently serves on the stake high council.

Mike struggled to get through my book because he saw it primarily as just another in a long line of books seeking to discredit the Mormon faith. It's not that he didn't find value in my analogies and explanations of the gospel of grace. What bothered him most was what he viewed as my attempt to downplay the role of grace in LDS theology, as well as intentionally placing emphasis on the role of obedience/works.

For weeks we e-mailed back and forth, seeking to dig deeper into the issues of salvation and, for the most part, clarifying our respective positions regarding grace; grace, plus works; etc. I would like to share portions of two e-mails in particular that I think go a long way to demonstrate the tone of this ongoing Mormon-Christian dialogue. In fact, I value these two exchanges so much that I decided to include them as an appendix.

In one e-mail, Mike sent me a quote from Apostle M. Russell Ballard in an effort to show me just how far the Church has come in valuing grace and, for added measure, to prove that I had misrepresented LDS teaching on this subject in my book. In the other, Mike comments on the "Hal and Tom" analogy from Chapter 5.

Elder Ballard's Quote

Elder Ballard wrote, "No matter how hard we work, no matter how much we obey, no matter how many good things we do in this life, it would never be enough were it not for Jesus Christ and His loving grace. On our own we cannot earn the kingdom of God, no matter what we do. Unfortunately, there are some within the Church who have become so preoccupied with performing good works that they forget that those works—as good as they may be—are hollow unless they are accompanied by a complete dependence on Christ."

—*Ensign*, June 1998, p. 65

My Response

There are so many subtleties to Elder Ballard's quote that I'm not sure where to begin. Let's break it down into three parts.

The first part reads, "No matter how hard we work … it would not be enough were it not for Jesus Christ and His loving grace." This is very much in harmony with LDS teaching. (And by the way, I sincerely hope I have not come across as insisting that Mormons believe ONLY in obedience and good works as their path to salvation. In my book I frequently refer to the combination of grace and works.) In effect, this first part of the quote is a restatement of the third Article of Faith.

The key word here is *enough*. This reinforces a key LDS doctrine (again, codified by the third Article of Faith) that obedience and good works make up a significant component of our salvation (eternal life in the celestial kingdom). Now, as to what percentage the obedience and good works represent in the overall salvation formula, that probably varies with every Latter-day Saint. You, for example [Mike], lean far more toward grace while acknowledging the importance of obedience.

But getting back to the first part of Elder Ballard's quote, the point is that he is referring to obedience and works in quantitative terms. It is not *enough*, in and of itself, "were it not for Jesus Christ …" I can't help but imagine a display or chart with zero at the bottom and 100 at the top (representing eternal life in the celestial kingdom). Kind of like something you'd see at a fund raiser where they have to hit some target to achieve their objective. Anyway, zero implies no grace and no obedience/good works. One hundred indicates a good solid serving of obedience/works (let's say 38 or 42 or even 50%) and the other 62, 58, or 50% would represent God's grace. (I concede that few Mormons, if any, ever talk of obedience/works as representing greater than 50% of the equation.) And in some cases, as in Stephen Robinson's bicycle analogy in *Believing Christ*, the actual contribution that our best efforts make is really a pittance compared to the overall "cost" of our salvation.

But here is the Christian response. We don't talk about obedience and good works as playing *any* role whatsoever in our salvation. None. There are no percentages because there is no chart (to account for any ratio of grace and obedience). **In fact, there is no fund raiser because the funds have already been raised!** Christ purchased our salvation when He died on the cross. And our debt to God (because of our sinfulness and inability to always do good works) was paid in full. *Tetelestai*!

This is the central theme of the entire New Testament—Christ dying on the cross was a total game changer! This message, of course, was very necessary for the Jews at the time. They had been trusting in the Law of Moses for 1,500 years—and in their ability to obey it as their one and only path to fellowship with God. I can't even imagine how difficult this transition would have been for them. Just place my faith and trust in Jesus? Yep.

Remember, Paul wrote, "… that Gentiles, who did not pursue righteousness, attained righteousness, even the righteousness which is by faith; but Israel, pursuing a law of righteousness, did not arrive at that law. Why? Because they did not pursue it by faith, but as though it were by works. They stumbled over the stumbling stone" (Ro 9:30–32).

And modern Mormons? Sort of hybrid Gentile/Jews in my opinion. Pursuing righteousness by faith *and* works. Such a little word, *and*. But [Mike], the *and* was at the very heart of what we call the "error of the Judaizers"—early Jewish converts to Christ who sought to reinsert the Law into salvation by grace (made possible by the cross).

On to the second part of Elder Ballard's quote: "Unfortunately, there are some within the Church who have become so preoccupied with performing good works …" All I can really say here, [Mike], is that I am encouraged by this little tidbit. It shows me that someone of Elder Ballard's stature (and authority) acknowledges that one's preoccupation with good works is problematic. **Let's face it, every minute we spend on this earth preoccupied by our own good works, is a minute we are not consciously worshipping God for His amazing Son who died so that we could live!** The Bible tells us that the BEST way to remain obedient to God's commandments and the ONLY way to truly do good works (from a place of love a la 1 Corinthians 13) is to continually abide in, meditate on, and rejoice in Christ's loving sacrifice. I think this is why Paul, late in his ministry, wrote, "For I have determined to know nothing among you except Jesus Christ, and Him crucified" (1 Cor 2:2).

However, don't you find Elder Ballard's lament a bit ironic? If we define salvation (to the LDS) as eternal life in the presence of God (i.e. celestial kingdom), then we must admit that in order to achieve that level of glory, one must receive all the blessings and covenants that come with the endowment in the temple. But in order to enter into the temple initially (and attend the temple regularly), one must have a temple recommend. But in order to have and maintain a temple recommend, one must be obedient and do many, if not most, of the very "good works" to which Elder Ballard is referring! And this is one of my main points, [Mike]:the Church has codified (by the third Article of Faith) and institutionalized over many years, the very thing that I call "Jesus Plus." Yes, Jesus Christ and Him crucified ... *plus* ... tithing, church attendance, word of wisdom, testimony of Joseph Smith, etc. Now, you may find the term "Jesus Plus" crude or disrespectful. Believe me, I REALLY find it disrespectful. But can you acknowledge that Mormonism, at its very core, is a form of "Jesus Plus"?

Finally, Elder Ballard says, "... those works—as good as they may be—are hollow unless they are accompanied by a **complete dependence** on Jesus Christ." I like this quote very much, all the way up to the word *hollow*. Our works are hollow, [Mike]. In fact, they're worse than hollow. They are used menstrual cloths—"filthy rags." Human works and "righteousness" will never even register on God's radar of immense glory and holiness. Of course this opens up another discussion of who God is and why the Christian feels far more inclined to just fall flat on his face before this magnificent God who has always been God, from everlasting to everlasting. My theory (and my experience as a LDS) is that the Mormon lacks the "Wow factor" in his feelings toward God, since God to him was once a man just like us! But I don't want to go down that lengthy road right now. Maybe some other time.

What I find fascinating is Ballard's use of the words "complete dependence." What he's saying is that good works are hollow (meaningless) unless they are accompanied by a complete dependence on Christ. **Yet, placing value (any value) on good works is, at its very core, an exercise in NOT placing one's complete dependence on Christ!** It's as if he's stepping up to the roulette wheel and telling the dealer (or whatever you call him), "Okay, I want to put ALL my money on black 17. And then I want to put this little bit of money on red 28." So when Elder Ballard talks about complete dependence, does he really mean *complete* dependence? No. Certainly not in the way I've learned to depend completely on Christ.

The "Hal and Tom" Analogy

Mike wrote:

> I like this parable. I would have no problems sharing it myself in a sacrament meeting. I would likely use it to teach the absolute necessity of the *atonement* of Christ. I acknowledge that we use the word atonement rather broadly in our teachings. It is meant to embrace the gift of Jesus' sacrifice on the cross as well as the suffering he endured in the Garden. I like the way the Protestants just wrap up the whole package using the word *grace*.
>
> I would use it to teach much of what you teach and would find it helpful to make the following points:
>
> 1. We are "natural men" who struggle to receive the things of the Spirit (1 Cor 2:14), who are "an enemy to God since the fall of Adam and will be forever and ever" (Mosiah 3:19). I would further emphasize our "nothingness" before God.
> 2. We have no hope of making it to shore, no matter how well we swim, unless we submit to God recognizing that only He has the power to save us.
> 3. **I would probably emphasize that it is important to at least start swimming**: show your love to Christ by repenting and keeping his commandments. I would NEVER suggest that one individual is a better swimmer than another because he does more good works. Good works does not equate to swimming ability! (I know that you later equate the water with the law—but the message that seems to keep coming from your book is that obedience to law is the same as good works, so it is hard for me to not feel over and over that you are condemning any effort at good works.) Swimming ability would only be repenting and following Christ. **For me there is no distance that we could swim to reach God, it is infinite. Just show that you are swimming and he lifts you up out of the water.**

I find Mike's commentary on the "Hal and Tom" analogy to be an excellent summation of LDS theology regarding salvation—precisely what I would have expected from him. Points one and two are very much in alignment with Bible teaching and constitute two of the areas of doctrinal overlap that often lead the Latter-day Saint to cry out in frustration, "See? We're Christian too! Why can't you evangelicals accept us?"

Point three, however, is where the Mormon and the Christian go their separate ways; although, in this case, it's where these two *swim* in completely opposite directions!

According to Mike, when the boat that Hal and Tom are on capsizes, and the Coast Guard arrives (with flotation devices to save them), their best option is to start swimming … to shore! Only when they "show that they are swimming" will the Guard toss in the life preservers and haul them up on to the deck. Is *this* what Nephi had in mind when he wrote, "… for we know that it is by grace that we are saved, after all we can do" (2 Nephi 25:23)? It appears so.

The Christian says, "Yeah, I'll start swimming … straight for the life preserver that the Coast Guard just tossed my way!"

You see, to the Christian, the important thing is to get out of the rough waters and into the safety and security of the boat. Once the Coast Guard takes us into shore, there will plenty of time to swim and snorkel and play around in the safe confines of the bay! This recreational swimming represents our "freedom in Christ."

Clearly, Jesus Christ is the Coast Guard in this analogy, and His cross is the life preserver. The Christian sees no benefit whatsoever in even *starting to* swim for shore. He immediately grabs hold of the cross and never lets it go. The Mormon thinks he's pleasing the Lord when he "at least starts swimming." Quite the contrary; Christ, from the deck of the boat, is calling out, "Where are you going? I'm right here!"